The Twelve Days of Christmas
ENCORE!

The Twelve Days of Christmas
ENCORE!

Easy Ideas for a More Memorable Christmas

BETTY VAN ORDEN

CFI
SPRINGVILLE, UT

This is not an official publication of The Church of Jesus Christ of Latter-day Saints. The opinions and views expressed herein belong solely to the author and do not necessarily represent the opinions or views of Cedar Fort, Inc. Permission for the use of sources, graphics, and photos is also solely the responsibility of the author.

ISBN 13: 978-1-59955-338-2

Published by CFI, an imprint of Cedar Fort, Inc., 2373 W. 700 S., Springville, UT 84663
Distributed by Cedar Fort, Inc., www.cedarfort.com

LIBRARY OF CONGRESS CATALOGING-IN-PUBLICATION DATA

Van Orden, Betty, 1943-
  The twelve days of Christmas encore! / Betty Van Orden.
    p. cm.
  Crafts, recipes, and other Christmas activities.
  ISBN 978-1-59955-338-2
  1. Christmas--Miscellanea. I. Title.

  GT4985.V333 2009
  394.2663--dc22

2009013030

Cover design by Nicole Williams
Cover design © 2009 by Lyle Mortimer
Edited and typeset by Melissa J. Caldwell

Printed in the United States of America

10 9 8 7 6 5 4 3 2 1

Printed on acid-free paper

*To my incredible husband, Sterling, who fills
each day of my life with beautiful memories.
I love you!*

OTHER BOOKS BY BETTY VAN ORDEN

The Twelve Days of Christmas—Ideas for a More Meaningful Holiday Season

Contents

Preface

Oh, parents, we would plead, give good and happy memories to your children—not pampering or over indulging, not satisfying everything they take a fancy to—but memories of love, encouragement, of peace and harmony and happiness at home—memories that will bless and lift their lives wherever they are, always and forever.

L. TOM PERRY

Thank you to each person who responded so beautifully to my book, *The Twelve Days of Christmas—Ideas for a More Meaningful Holiday Season.* Your comments gave me great hope that we *are* giving more meaning to this glorious season of the year. My heart was full as I read the experiences you had while embracing this idea. Each card, letter, email, and phone call was inspiring and precious to me. Tears have flooded my eyes as I read your stories and felt the tremendous love you have shown your families. Isn't it incredible how quickly the spirit of service fills our hearts? As I said before, it's amazing what the *mind* can do when the *heart* is involved. And didn't it feel amazing? There just isn't much that compares to serving our family. Sharing this with you has been more than I could ever have dreamed it would be.

For those of you who are new to this concept, let me tell you a little about this special gift-giving for twelve days. You will begin by choosing a theme for your 12 Days of Christmas. It should be one that suits your family—perhaps a theme that will encourage your family in an area in which they may need to be strengthened. Select gifts—one for each day—that will blend with your theme. Write a note explaining the gift and place it on the inside of the package before it is wrapped. After wrapping your gift, place a number on the outside so the recipient will know on which day they are to open that particular gift. We place all our gifts in a Tupperware bin with a lid. Each day the family goes to the big Tupperware container and takes out the gift numbered for that day. Prepare a cover letter telling your family or friends about the theme you have chosen and also instructing them as to what you want them to do. We are able to deliver powerful messages through this way of gift-giving. This book is about lessons shared and learned while serving those we love.

Some of you chose to reflect on each of the themes in my previous book to see which ones would fit your family best. There must have been times when you had to decide which things you could do and which things you would want to do differently. That's what makes this all so wonderful! You can choose what's best for *you* to do! Listen closely as the Spirit speaks to your heart and mind. You will know exactly what is needed for your individual families. Many of you have already experienced this inspiration and know what I'm talking about.

Michael McLean, the popular song writer, made the following statement: "Song writers know that they don't really own the songs they've written . . . they just hear them first." We are much like this as we prepare our themes and gifts for those we care about. We don't claim to "own" the idea . . . we just own the desire! We may hear the ideas first because we are listening.

Because of the tremendous response I received from you, I have decided to open my heart and share additional thoughts and ideas. My hope is to bring an even stronger desire to make Christmas all it can and should be within our families. I'm excited to have you join me for another series of themes, thoughts, gifts, stories, poems, patterns, and recipes. I'll try to light a spark within you so you'll be "off and running" to get your 12 Days of Christmas started for another year.

Introduction

I wish we all had a room in our homes where we could keep Christmas all year. For most of us, this is near to impossible. But think about it . . . what if we had a room in which we kept our Christmas tree decorated and the soft lights on. The ornaments we had so carefully chosen for our tree would still be hanging beautifully, and it would be as magnificent as during the holidays. Carefully, oh so carefully, we would lift an ornament, hold it tenderly in our hands, and remember the beauty it had added to our tree.

And in that same room, what if we could sit by a warm fireplace and listen to the crackling of the logs and to our favorite Christmas carols? The smell of fresh pine would fill the air and we would be at peace in our special room. We would have the Christmas afghan, which we had received as a gift, laying over our favorite chair. As we sat there, we would use it to cover our legs just as we had done during those wonderful days of Christmas. Memories of a loved one would flood our minds as we thought how tenderly she had presented this gift to us and the many hours she had spent preparing it. It would always be a treasure!

The walls would be covered with pictures of holidays spent with those we love. Perhaps a few pictures are of our own children when they were young, showing the excitement they always displayed at the thought of Santa's arrival. On another wall would be pictures of grandchildren sitting on Santa's lap, smiling that timid little smile they always seem to have when they visit Santa. Pictures of friends would be there as well, friends both new and old, and pictures of other loved ones who bring joy to our lives and fill our hearts with beautiful memories. On the table would be a stack of Christmas books inviting us to browse their pages. We could now choose a book and read for as long as we desired. Occasionally, we would lay our heads back and let our minds wander to the hustle and bustle of Christmas, and we might even spend some time planning how different next year is going to be! We would set aside some time to thank our Heavenly Father in prayer for allowing us to experience the celebration of the birth of His Son with those we love most.

These thoughts would bring to mind the Nativity, the focus of our celebration. We would recall the happy days when we were newly married and shopped for hours in search of the perfect nativity. Money was limited, so we chose carefully. It has always held a special place in our hearts. We tenderly caress each figure and remember the many years it has held a special place in our home. Years later we purchased the more magnificent nativity when finances allowed us that privilege. There is the bag of straw we sat beside the manger. This was used by our family to soften the bed for baby Jesus. With each good deed we performed, we placed a piece of straw in the manger. If we were faithful in our efforts, we would have provided a soft bed for the baby on Christmas Eve.

Oh, this would be the most amazing room! It would be a refuge for our hearts when they needed to be softened because they had become hardened and angry from the affairs of the world. It would help ease aching hearts that had suffered sorrow, grief, and pain. It would help bring joy where loneliness had crept in. I would love to have such a room in my home but I believe that *memories* can provide such a room within our own hearts. If we take time in the rush of life to ponder the Christmas that is in our heart, then perhaps we can have this special "refuge." We can each return at will to Christmas any time of the year. In fact, I think I'm going to go there for a short while right now. I'm in need of some relaxing time where I'll remember the beautiful tree my husband and I decorated together. I'll listen for soft Christmas carols we played as we decorated our home and, yes, now and then one of us would be singing a little louder than usual. Laughter fills the room and memories are made. I'll think of those precious smiling faces of our children and grandchildren as they open "each day" of the 12 Days of Christmas. Anticipation grew for both Sterling and me until we could witness the excitement they showed with each gift. The phone calls and emails were priceless!

Where do you find more joy? I'm off to spend some time in my special room. Come along with me. I love sharing with a friend.

I've been busy making more memories during the past several years and I want to share them with you. Perhaps you will choose to use some of these ideas to make memories for that special Christmas room in your mind and heart.

Chapter One

Angels Among Us

What you do enough of—you become!

UNKNOWN

This year had been an unusual one for us. We usually know exactly what we want our theme to be, but several themes seemed to fit our family. Because this was for the people we love most, we knew the theme had to be just right. After much thought, prayer, and feeling the promptings in our hearts, we decided that our theme should be "Angels Among Us." Recalling the many acts of kindness and love we had observed during the past year helped us make our decision. I believe that most parents desire for their children to grow up to know the true love of Christ—service to others. We, as parents and grandparents, are often the recipients of these kind acts, and our hearts become full to overflowing. A perfect example was shown by our Savior through His sojourn here on earth. He showed us how we should live and how to serve one another. We expressed our gratitude to our family for the way they are living their lives and for becoming true angels on earth as they do good deeds for others. After all, we never know when we are acting as an angel in the life of someone else.

On the FIRST Day of

Christmas
We bring to you with love . . .

A beautiful nativity set! Let this serve as your "good deed" nativity. When you have performed a good deed for someone, you may put a piece of straw in the manger to help make a softer bed for the baby Jesus. By serving others we are following the teachings of Jesus. We have also included the book, *The Last Straw*, for you to read together as a family.

In addition, we are including a small box with a paper inside. You are to write on the paper a gift you can give to *Jesus* this year. For example, you might choose to be a peacemaker in your home during the holidays by using only kind words that are softly spoken, or you could be faithful in saying your prayers each day. Perhaps you desire to be a better helper to Mom and Dad during the holidays. The gift *you* give needs to come from your heart and be one you desire to give. After you have written your gift to Jesus on the paper, place the paper back in the box and place the box under your Christmas tree. On Christmas Eve you will take the box from under your tree, open it, and see if you have been successful in giving your promised gift to Jesus. When we follow the example of our Savior, it makes our gift special to Him. We are becoming angels on earth. And, yes, there *is* another part to Day #1 . . . NeNa's fudge! Enjoy every bite and remember how much love goes into making it for you!

Sterling and I searched many stores before finding what we felt was the perfect nativity for our families. We included a small bag of straw for them to use to soften the manger with their good deeds. A few phone calls were made before we found the pretty silver and gold boxes at a stationary store. They were the perfect size so all we needed to add was a small bow on top. It was a lovely box to hold their gift to Jesus. And the fudge . . . well, that's a story I shared in my first book. Our children and grandchildren tell everyone that their NeNa (the name I'm known by and Sterling is PaPa) makes the best fudge out of anyone! You don't get comments like that very often, so each year I make sure there is plenty of fudge on the first day of our 12 Days of Christmas. Some years I tease the grandchildren and tell them that this year I won't be making fudge, but they always comment,

"NeNa, we know you are only kidding with us. You know how much we love your
fudge!" What I hope they mean is that they know how very much I love each one
of them.

Day
#2

On the SECOND Day of

Christmas

We bring to you with love . . .

An Angel's Act of Service! First, listen to the CD, *Angels Among Us*,
which we have chosen to include today. The words to this song are especially
beautiful, and we hope you will listen to this song many times because it
has touched your hearts. Now for the next step! Think of a member of our
family whom you think could use extra prayers during the holidays. Pray
for this person and ask that you might be aware of the special blessings for
which they are in need. Pray for them every day—morning and night—from
now until Christmas Day. You *will* make a difference! Your prayers will be
heard, and you will be an angel in this person's life! This will bring the spirit
of Christmas into your life and blessings into the life of the person for whom
you are praying. It won't cost you any money . . . just your time and your love.
We all have time for this! Each of us can experience the joy of being an angel
in someone's life.

This proved to be one of the most beautiful memories ever. Each person
searched for the one on whom they would focus and for whom they would pray.
We couldn't have hoped for a more wonderful experience for our family. Putting
someone else and his needs before ourselves is something we wanted our grand-
children to experience. One of our children said, "I cried when I prayed. I knew
the person I chose would be very happy if they knew I was praying for them. I
love this person so much."

On the THIRD Day of
Christmas
We bring to you with love . . .

An Angel's Feather Memory Tree Ornament! The white feather inside the clear plastic ball is to represent an angel's feather. We each have many angels in our lives. Some of our angels no longer live here on the earth, but we believe in our hearts that they continue to love and watch over us. The words written on the little tag attached to the ball tell that this is a feather from an angel. Its purpose is to serve as a reminder of a special person's love, who is now your Guardian Angel and watches over you from up above. We pray you will always have angels in your lives. Oh, how we love you!

❄ ❄ ❄ ❄ ❄

I was very fortunate to find these angel ornaments in a popular craft magazine. It's full of wonderful gifts to use in planning your 12 Days of Christmas. Even though we believe angels don't have feathers, the feather seemed to represent the purity and softness of an angel. The ornaments came unassembled so I enjoyed putting them together, knowing how each family was going to love them. Indeed, they were exactly what I was looking for and they helped enforce the teachings that we do have angels watching over us from heaven. The ornaments came with white glitter to sprinkle over the feather to make it even more beautiful. One granddaughter commented to her mother, "Mommy, do you think there is someone in heaven watching over me? I hope I have a guardian angel." What a perfect teaching time for us as parents and grandparents.

On the FOURTH Day of
Christmas
We bring to you with love . . .

An Evening with NeNa and PaPa! Tonight you are invited to spend a fun evening with NeNa and PaPa at our home. Plan to arrive at 6:30 for a wonderful evening. We will be watching the Christmas movie *It's* *a Wonderful Life* with Jimmy Stewart, plus we will be having some delicious snacks. We can hardly wait to spend time with each one of you. You bring such happiness to our lives!

❄ ❄ ❄ ❄ ❄

I used my cookie cutters to cut bread in angel shapes for sandwiches. I also baked some angel-shaped sugar cookies to serve to our "special" guests along with a cup of warm cocoa. Your imagination will run wild as you think of the many things you can prepare using this theme. Angel food cake is another delicious dessert when topped with some berries and whipping cream. Some people drizzle a little chocolate over the berries. Yum!

On the FIFTH Day of

Christmas
We bring to you with love . . .

An Angel Pitcher and New Books! We hope this will be a fun day for you and that you will especially enjoy reading these new books about angels and how they can touch our lives. We're learning lots about angels this year, aren't we? Don't forget to ask mommy to put something yummy in your beautiful angel pitcher to drink while you read your books. We know how you love chocolate milk!

❄ ❄ ❄ ❄ ❄

We knew this was a theme that was definitely going to be used in one of our 12 Days of Christmas in the future, so we began looking early for anything pertaining to angels. We loved the pitchers with beautiful angels painted on them. These were a huge hit with each family. A good time to look for these is the day after Thanksgiving sales. You may also want to use the Internet for finding unique gifts. It's such an easy way to shop, and most often you will find the item you want. It's always nice to have gifts delivered right to your door; plus, you don't have to spend time fighting the holiday crowds.

On the SIXTH Day of
Christmas
We bring to you with love . . .

Lollipops! Angel shaped lollipops to share with your friends this year! Remember to take one for you and one for your best friend. Perhaps this year you could tell your friend he or she is an "angel" in your life. Angels are people who make us happy and who are special in our lives. Friends are like that! We do love and cherish our friends.

> *Friends are kisses blown to us by angels.*
>
> UNKNOWN

✳ ✳ ✳ ✳ ✳

I was able to find angel lollipop molds in our local craft store and started making them early in the season, so they were ready to be delivered. Any gift that can be made ahead turns out to be a blessing. You can also find the flavorings, sticks, bags, and trimmings for lollipops in most craft stores. I used some gold cording to tie around the stick so it had more of an angelic look. Any day I can spend preparing gifts for our family truly fills my heart with joy.

On the SEVENTH Day of
Christmas
We bring to you with love . . .

A Beautiful Baking Dish and a New Journal! How excited we were when we saw this pretty red baking dish! Right away we knew we had to buy it for you. We are including a jar of cobbler mix, so you can bake a delicious treat for your family tonight. There's nothing better than a warm cobbler topped with ice cream! As you sit around the table enjoying the cobbler, we hope you will talk about the importance of keeping a journal. We have been encouraged to write down our thoughts at the end of each day and keep this record for ourselves and for our posterity. You might write about something wonderful that has happened to you, a trial you may have faced and how you handled that trial, a new friend you have made, or your feelings about where you are in life at this time. Definitely take time to write about the angels who surround you. Please make a commitment to write at least once a week. It will be a wonderful habit to acquire! We will be blessed for our efforts, because we are doing what we believe is important. Your journal will become a priceless treasure in your life.

❄ ❄ ❄ ❄ ❄

One of our greatest desires with the Twelve Days of Christmas is to help rein-force the good values we know our children are teaching in their homes. Realizing the value of keeping a daily journal, we hoped to convey this to our loved ones. Nice journals can be found at most stationary shops. The red baking dish was one we found after the holidays one year. We got a great buy on them and knew they would make a wonderful gift. Each mother commented that she never seems to have enough attractive baking dishes, so she especially appreciated receiving a new one. We found the cobbler mix in a local Cracker Barrel restaurant, which has a darling gift shop attached. The choices were great! You could always make your own cobbler mix, if you choose. Just be sure you deliver it fresh.

On the EIGHTH Day of

Christmas

We bring to you with love . . .

A Treasure Box and CD! Won't this look beautiful on a special shelf or table in your office or family room? It even has a clock on the outside so it is especially unique. Perhaps this is a perfect "time" for us to talk about the "treasures" in our lives. How many can you name? Have you mentioned your friends, family, teachers, or the angels who make our lives more wonderful? We are very blessed and have many treasures for which we should be thankful. We are also including a CD made by the sons and daughters of two of our dearest friends, Bruno and Cari Vassel. Their family has been blessed with wonderful musical talent, and they made this special CD to share with friends and family during this time of the year. Listen closely to the words of the song "Will He Really Answer Me?" We want you to know that we believe our Heavenly Father does hear and answer our every prayer. Prayer is truly one of our treasures.

✶ ✶ ✶ ✶ ✶

We found the treasure box in a local décor shop and were delighted with it. You can probably find something similar in your local franchise stores or on the Internet. The box was made of leather with a small clock on the outside. It fit beautifully in the home of each family. Who doesn't like something new to help decorate our homes after the holidays?

On the NINTH Day of

Christmas

We bring to you with love . . .

A Special Picture for You! This framed picture of you with your cousins is for you to set where you will appreciate it most. It was taken at your Aunt Julie's wedding this past summer when you were all dressed up in your gorgeous outfits. Cousins truly are angels in our lives. We watch you as you play. You have lots of fun together, and you care for one another. We hope you will always cherish the friendships of family and realize what a blessing you are to one another. Try always to build on family ties and allow angels to be with you.

✶ ✶ ✶ ✶ ✶

Sterling got all the grandchildren together and took pictures so we would have lots to choose from for this special surprise. We tried to make this fun for all the cousins by using scrapbook paper that enhanced the pictures. We watched for sales on picture frames and found ones that were especially great for children. These were a big hit with the grandchildren, and they shared with us how much they love their cousins. Truly, this was no surprise to us!

On the TENTH Day of

Christmas
We bring to you with love . . .

A New Christmas Mug! We found these mugs in beautiful Christmas colors. We have added the theme for the year to the mugs: *Angels Among Us.* This way you will be reminded of our theme throughout the remainder of this season and into the next year. We know how much you love hot chocolate, so we have included a can of your favorite flavor. We hope your life will always be full of happiness and joy just as your cup is full today. Remember how much you are loved!

Often you don't have to look long and hard to find exactly what you want. Angel themes seem to be quite popular and we found several beautiful mugs. Gold colored permanent markers were used to write our theme on the cups in a fancy font. They turned out darling! The cups helped to express how much we desire to bless our families' lives.

On the ELEVENTH Day of

Christmas
We bring to you with love . . .

An Evening of Christmas Caroling! Tonight is going to be very special for our family. We will meet at NeNa's and PaPa's home at 7:00 and plan to be caroling by 7:15. Be sure to dress warmly with hats, gloves, and boots. We wouldn't want you to get cold! Several people in our neighborhood are alone during the holidays, and some have recently returned from a stay in the hospital. They will appreciate us visiting them and singing some of our favorite Christmas carols. It's a wonderful way to bring our family together with the true spirit of Christmas, and perhaps we will be angels in the lives of the people we visit. We look forward to spending time with you tonight. And, yes, we will top off the evening with some hot cider and donuts when we finish our caroling.

❄ ❄ ❄ ❄ ❄

Is there anything more beautiful than the sound of children's voices! It's a perfect evening when you can be together with your family and also feel you are bringing special joy to others as you visit with them. We didn't make this a long evening since we have several smaller children. Many hearts were touched by the sweet voices of our angels, our children and grandchildren.

On the TWELFTH Day of

Christmas

We bring to you with love . . .

A set of Angel Chimes! As you know, PaPa loves chimes, so when he saw these in a shop in West Yellowstone, he wanted each of the families to have a set. Finding the chimes with these adorable angels on them was especially exciting for us. They were bought and tucked away for the perfect time to present them to you. Today is that "perfect" day! May you each be reminded of the angels in your lives as you hear soft sounds ringing from the chimes throughout the year. *You* are true angels in our lives.

❄ ❄ ❄ ❄ ❄

What a hit these chimes were! The grandchildren often express how they think of the angels in their lives when they hear the tinkling sounds of the chimes. Many stores carry chimes. You may also want to check at some specialty shops or on the Internet.

Earth's Angels

The dim glare from the light poles left the parking lot shrouded in darkness. Some of the staff had attempted to brighten the nursing home with Christmas lights, but it was obvious to anyone visiting that decorating was not their forté. There were only a few cars in the parking lot because most of the workers wouldn't arrive for several hours. As I hurried from my car toward the nursing home, my heart raced so fast I could hear it pounding in my head. The dreaded call I received in the wee hours of the morning repeated over in my head. "Emily," the familiar voice called out, "you need to get here as soon as possible. Your dad isn't doing well, and we promised to call if there was any change. His temperature is elevated and the infection is rapidly spreading throughout his body."

The urgency of the nurse's voice caused me to tremble as I quickly dressed and prepared to leave for the nursing home. "David," I whispered softly in my husband's ear, "wake up! The nurse called and we need to get to Dad right away."

I have been blessed with a good marriage and a strong husband who is always by my side. We are as much in love today as we were the day we married. The love of such an incredible man has been the force behind many of my successes in life. I knew I would need him by my side during the coming days.

David held my hand tightly as we hurried down the hall to Dad's room. I rushed to my father's side and tenderly took his hand in mine. He looked so feeble lying there in his bed. I placed my other hand on his forehead and immediately ascertained that his temperature had soared since I had last seen him.

"Dad," I said as I struggled to get the words out, "Dad, can you hear me? It's me, Emily . . . I came as quickly as I could. I'm here with you and so is David." David had always been one of Dad's favorite people. In his eyes David could do no wrong. Dad had been especially proud when David was called to be the bishop of our ward. "There is no finer man anywhere," he boasted. "My daughter married a wonderful man."

My sweet husband had always been good to Dad and was happy when he received a phone call from Dad asking if he would come by and take him for a ride. Any distraction would do. He needed to get out of the house—and away from the loneliness he felt since Mother's death. Dad welcomed visitors and was quick to challenge them to a game of checkers. Those who accepted the challenge never let him win, but Dad always managed to emerge victorious. Dad's laughter echoed down the halls and made even the most hardened nurse smile. Dementia hadn't slowed his game at all, but his desire to play had diminished during the past several months. It seemed Dad was losing interest in the things that had once meant so much.

Scott, one of the hospice nurses, came toward me with outstretched hands. "Emily, you know I love your dad. Remember I'm here for you, too. I'll be checking on you both throughout the day. Be strong for him."

The day dragged on as I watched Dad labor for each breath without respite. His suffering was much like that of a mother laboring to bring forth her newborn baby, but without the relief that comes between contractions. "Oh, Daddy," I cried, "your mouth is so dry." I moistened the sponge and wet his lips, tongue, and the inside of his mouth. It seemed to bring some relief, if only for a few moments. It helped me to be able to serve him during this last day of his life on earth.

Tears flowed gently down my face when the hospice nurse entered the room. "It won't be long now," he said. "Your father has reached the end of his life and his body is beginning to shut down in preparation for the release of the spirit. His body isn't strong enough to house his spirit any more. I believe, from my experience, that he will not suffer much longer."

As Dad's final hours approached, many workers and staff members stopped by to extend their sympathies. "I know this isn't new to you," I said. "You must witness the passing of many patients, but somehow you make me feel that my dad is special to you." Linda, my dad's favorite nurse, commented, "Your father is a happy man. He never complains even when I know he is in pain. Instead, he will extend his hand and warmly thank me for each thing I do to make his day a little better." That's the way Dad was; perhaps, it was the southern gentleman coming through. Another nurse overheard and added, "Your dad always asks about my family. One of my sons is crippled and confined to a wheelchair. Occasionally, my husband brings Ty to the nursing home for a visit. Your father always enjoyed talking with Ty and always gave him some candy to take home. I want you to know that his kindness has meant a lot to me and my husband."

"Thank you for sharing this with me," I said, wiping the tears from my eyes.

When David and I were once again alone with Dad, I recognized a peaceful feeling in the room. "Dad," I whispered, "I think the angels must be nearby. Your mother and father must be anticipating your arrival. You have been apart from them for many years and your relationship with your parents was very special. I know there will be a joyous reunion." *How excited my grandmother will be to hold her son once again,* I thought to myself. *Is she watching him now—lying here laboring for breath—so frail and feeble? She, too, must be shedding tears as she anticipates the return of her son.* My thoughts turned to our Savior as I pictured the joy of His reunion with my dad.

When Scott returned to check Dad's vital signs, he turned to me and softly said, "Emily, your dad's hearing will be the last of his senses to leave him, so continue talking to him throughout the day. It will be important for your dad to hear your voice."

Oh, how I would like my last words to my father to be special. I wondered what I could say that would cheer his soul. And then a memory surfaced. I remembered the Sunday afternoon drives we took when I was a child. I always sat in the seat behind my dad. We didn't have seat belts then, so I sometimes stood behind him and talked to him while he was driving. Many times he spent the entire trip teaching me how to spell so I would be the best speller in my class. He also taught me the little poem that became dear to my heart. "Dad, do you remember the poem you taught me when I was just a little girl? Do you remember, 'Come Little Leaves'?" A slight smile crossed his face, or perhaps it was just my wishful thinking. That poem became a special link between the two of us and sometimes a few years would pass before one of us would say to the other, "Bet you don't remember 'Come Little Leaves'?" Then we would recite together.

> *"Come little leaves," said the wind one day,*
> *"Come over the meadows with me and play;*
> *Put on your dresses of red and gold,*
> *Summer is gone, and the days grow cold."*
> *Dancing and flying the little leaves went*
> *Winter had called them, and they were content,*
> *Soon, fast asleep in their earthly beds*
> *The snow laid a coverlet over their heads.*
>
> GEORGE COOPER

His breathing calmed a little. I was happy that I had brought a few moments of comfort to my dear father, but the lump in my throat was choking me. I wanted to cry . . . the kind of crying you do in a locked room and you pray no one is near. The reality that this was Dad's last day was sinking into my head but not into my heart. I was going to be alone without either of my parents. My heart was breaking!

I heard the sound of Christmas carols coming from the next room. Some young girls had come to sing to the residents in the nursing home. The music gave me an idea that I should sing to Dad. He always loved music and he often sang along with his favorite artists on the radio. I leaned close to his ear and softly sang some carols and then I sang a favorite hymn that reminds us that families can be together forever. My singing leaves a lot to be desired, but it didn't matter today. It was just my daddy and me. I knew he would like it.

Just a few months before, I had attended church with Dad at the nursing home. Dementia had become a big problem in his life, and sometimes he didn't recognize me nor did he recall things I thought should be fresh in his mind. That Sunday, as we began to sing hymns, I leaned over to Dad and asked him to sing along with me. In only a few moments he was singing hymns that he had loved for many years. He remembered every word! Oh, what a joy that was to hear him sing once again. One of God's tender mercies to me!

Is he thinking how short his life span had been or is he remembering the many years of struggle and hard work he faced? I wondered. Life hadn't always been easy for him. I remember Mother telling the story of his teenage years when his father became very ill and could no longer work to support his family. Dad had quit school and gone to work so that his mother would be able to care for her children. Dad found a job that paid $10.75 a week. Back then this was considered to be a good-paying job. He gave his mother ten dollars and he kept seventy-five cents for himself. That tells a lot about the love he had for his family. I never remember a visit to my grandparents' home when Dad wouldn't rush immediately to his mother and give her a big hug. He truly loved her.

"Oh, Dad," I exclaimed. "Do you remember how beautiful Mother was when you two got married? You always told everyone that you married the most beautiful woman in the world! We all knew this was true." Mom and Dad were together for more than fifty years before Mother had a stroke and was hospitalized. It had now been more than fourteen years since her death. That's a long time to be without the one you love.

"Dad, you were very young when you were drafted into the army. Did you fear that you would be forced to take the life of another person in order to defend your own life in battle? You were brave to leave your family and your homeland to go to a foreign country to fight against boys your own age. Did I ever thank you enough for your sacrifice?" I could hardly speak, for tears were choking me. Dad talked little of those years. Mother always said it was too painful for him. War is a terrible thing!

Remembering the purple heart Dad had received after being wounded in the Battle of the Bulge, I told him once again how proud I was that he had fought for our country's freedom. "I will always cherish your purple heart," I said with pride. "You said you wanted your grandson, Jon, to have it some-day. I will make sure your wishes are fulfilled. Your wounded leg—a shot by an enemy soldier—has been the cause of many years of pain and suffering. I'm so sorry, Dad . . . thank you!"

The room began to fill with family members who wanted to say good-bye to their grandfather. "Dad," I said, "your grandchildren are here. They want to express their love to you."

Our children knew grandpa had taken a turn for the worse the past week so they weren't surprised when they received the call telling them Grandpa had reached the end of his life's mission. Each one gave love and support to me and said their farewells to Grandpa. A precious daughter whispered in my ear, "Mother, our family believes families can be together forever, and you must hold tight to this knowledge. It will sustain you during this difficult time. Grandpa is going to a better life where there are no painful wounded legs and no more reaching out for breath to sustain life."

The nurses checked on us regularly. "Emily," one nurse tenderly called, "your dad has brought so much fun and laughter to those around him. His quick wit and keen sense of humor have cheered us on many gloomy days. Oh, yes, often his jokes would be the same ones he had told before, but we would have a good laugh together, and I always went away feeling better." She then administered Dad's medications and repositioned him, hoping to have made him a little more comfortable. I was assured he was as comfortable as they could possibly make him. I loved the nurses for their unselfish service. *Help me to learn from their examples that I too need to be as compassionate with others.*

"Honey, how are you holding up?" David asked as he held me in his arms. "I think the end is near." Dad's labored breathing increased and then it began to slow a little and I knew that he was approaching the end.

"Daddy, I'm here. You're not alone. I promise not to leave you. It's okay, Daddy. . . . It's okay to let go. I love you. Don't worry about me. I have my wonderful family for support. Many await you on the other side and there will be a joyous reunion. Go quietly into the kingdom that awaits you and kiss my sweet mother for me. I will miss you both every day. And, Dad, please watch over my children for me. I love them so much. "

Dad's breaths became fewer and fewer . . . then one final breath. His earthly mission was completed. He was at peace.

No . . . please . . . no . . . I need more time! I know I was supposed to be preparing myself for this final moment but I'm not ready . . . let me learn more; let me gain more strength . . . help me. No one heard the silent cries within me. Nurses came from every direction. Each seemed to know exactly what to do. Some consoled me while others tended to Dad's body and all that was required at that time.

My own body felt numb. Outside the snow was piling up, and it appeared to be extremely cold. Inside, I searched for some comfort and something to make my pain go away. I prayed. Where else could I turn? And then the angels came! Suddenly I felt our son, Jason, place his arms around me offering me a shoulder to lean on when I was hardly able to stand. What a blessing to have children who are sensitive, loving, and kind.

Somehow I made it through the next few days. During this time, I was surrounded by my husband and children as they showered me with acts of kindness and love. It was good to not be alone. When they *had* to be gone, I knew they were only a phone call away. Julie made her daily phone calls to say, " I love you, Mom." It's amazing how the sound of a loved one's voice can lift our spirits and give us strength to make it through another day.

After meeting with the funeral director, we were surprised to return to a beautifully cleaned home. One of our precious daughters made sure everything had been dusted, vacuumed, and given a shine. People would be arriving from out of town, and she knew they would be spending time at our home. "Oh, Heather," I exclaimed, "how is it that you always seem to be aware of the needs of others. Thank you, thank you!"

Before Dad had become so ill, I had agreed to be the guest speaker at several ladies' group meetings. It was too late to cancel, so I put forth my best effort to make sure I was prepared for each of the meetings. I arrived home one evening after a long night and found on the kitchen counter a tub of homemade caramel corn with a note that read, "Enjoy one of your favorite treats after a long day and know our love and thoughts are with you. Love, Jon and Jill." How sweet of our younger son and his wife to think of me amid all they had going on in their own lives. How easy they are to love!

The telephone was ringing as we rushed into the house from making more preparations for Dad's funeral. "Mom," Stephanie said, "we prepared a hot meal for you and Dad. Come right over." She continued such acts of kindness for many more evenings. We were overwhelmed with our daughter's compassion.

The day of the funeral came more quickly than I had wanted. The room was filling with those who wished to pay their last respects. Many had chosen to send lovely Christmas plants and arrangements. I felt as though I were watching from another room. Nothing seemed real as I went through the motions. The funeral services were about to begin when our children presented me with a lovely corsage of yellow roses. "We know they were grandmother's favorite flowers," Kaye said softly, "and we want you to wear them next to your heart today to remind you she is here in spirit".

"Oh," I cried, "how did you ever think of this? It means the world to me to have my mother so close to my heart today."

Each speaker seemed to have carefully chosen his or her words and with deep feeling. I clung to every word as a first-grader clings to the hem of his mother's dress on the first day of school. Tears flowed down my eleven-year-old granddaughter's cheeks as she recited, "Come Little Leaves." She could hardly speak. My first instinct was to go to her, so I left my seat and quickly made it to the podium. "Brianne, let's recite the poem together," I whispered quietly. She gave me one of her incredible smiles; then, arm in arm, we recited the words of the poem, and I felt my dad was listening to every word. He loved these precious grandchildren. Some of them had hidden their faces with their tiny hands as emotions took over. Their good-byes had taken place a few weeks before when they came to the nursing home, but now it seemed so final. Grandpa had taken each child in his arms and told them of his deep love for them and offered a gentle reminder to always do what they know is right. Memories of that evening were touching their hearts. *We never know when final memories are being made.*

The funeral ended and I watched as the pall bearers carefully placed the casket in the hearse. We walked the short distance to the gravesite. The day was cold but calm with a promise of snow in the forecast. Suddenly, out of nowhere, a puff of wind blew a bundle of leaves high into the air in front of me. To my surprise, all those around me cried out, "Come little leaves! Oh, Emily, this is amazing."

It was true! Dad had found a way to say. "Bet you don't remember 'Come Little Leaves.' "

I believe Dad wanted me to know his spirit still lives and that he loves me and appreciates all I have done for him. Oh, how sweet are the tender mercies of a loving Heavenly Father who watches over our every need and desire.

Looking around at the many wreaths which had been placed on the graves, Christmas seemed, indeed, a special time to remember those who meant so much to us and played an important part in our lives.

Ever felt an angel's breath in the gentle breeze?
a teardrop in the falling rain?
Hear a whisper amongst the rustle of leaves?

or been kissed by a lone snowflake?
Nature is an angel's favorite hiding place.

Carrie Latet

My husband and I have presented the 12 Days of Christmas to our family for quite a few years, and we weren't about to stop now. We all felt such a tremendous amount of love in our family. We always have a theme for our 12 Days of Christmas—one that we feel will be special for our family. I was concerned that I wasn't going to be able to think of a meaningful theme in such a short time plus prepare the gifts for each day. Somehow the decorating, baking, and shopping would get done. I'd make sure of it!

After driving home in a blinding snow storm, I was surprised to see my two daughters-in-law pulling out of our driveway. They had cute but suspicious grins on their faces. "There just might be a surprise waiting for you!" Kelly shouted as they pulled away. I raced into the house with the excitement of a youngster on Christmas morning. What had these two Christmas Elves been up to? As I entered the family room, my eyes quickly turned to see the most amazing Christmas tree fully decorated with the new ornaments I had purchased. "Oh my!" I shouted. My husband was standing in the next room watching as I experienced the joy of such a surprise. "Isn't the tree beautiful!" David exclaimed. "The girls wanted to help you and they felt this would be one way they could."

Morning seemed to arrive much too quickly. My body wanted more rest, but I knew I had lots to accomplish and needed to get the day started. I sat by the Christmas tree, looking out at the freshly fallen snow. It had laid a lovely blanket over our yard. I've always loved the warmth and coziness snow brings. As I recalled the many Christmas holidays in the past, memories of my childhood filled my heart. Mother had a special way of making Christmas perfect in our home. There was always a beautifully decorated tree; soft, white lights on the trees outside; lots of delicious food cooking and filling the air with incredible smells of the holidays; logs on the fire; a nativity arranged perfectly so it could be seen by everyone who came to visit; and beautifully wrapped gifts. I cherish these memories. I wonder if David and I had provided treasured memories for our children. I want them to remember the Christmases in our home with joy in their hearts and thanksgiving for being blessed to live in a home where they *knew* they were loved. That is a wonderful gift to give a child. There should never be a doubt where love is concerned.

I'm not sure at what point the answer finally came, but all of a sudden, my heart was full to overflowing. Why of course . . . that was the perfect answer to my dilemma. How could I have been so blind! My own family members are truly angels to all those around them and I too had been the recipient of their good works. I was searching for a theme for our family for the 12 Days of Christmas, and all the time it had been right before me. Our children and grandchildren were showing through their good works that they had learned and, more important, were showing by example how *true* angels on earth should be. That was it! We would honor these angels in our lives this year. Our theme would be "Angels Among Us." We would celebrate the many angels who walk in and out of our lives as we experience the joys and the trials we must face on earth. The blessings of our Heavenly Father never seem to leave us. Wasn't Jesus the perfect example of love and service? Didn't He teach us how important it is to live His teachings that we may also inherit the kingdom of His Father? Our Savior's love always and forever will be so infinite that it includes every one of us.

Don't tell God how big your storm is,
tell the storm how big your God is.

AUTHOR UNKNOWN

Often we go in search of angels and miracles when they are right before us. It may have taken the softening of my heart through the death of my father to appreciate the angels who are within my own family. My Heavenly Father had sent these angels to grace my life. *I pray I will always appreciate who they are and help them to become all they can be.*

Did they realize when they were preparing the meals, cleaning our home, decorating the Christmas tree, pinning a corsage of yellow roses on their Mom, making daily phone calls to make sure Mom and Dad were okay, extending open arms of comfort, leaving special treats to show they care, and always showing their love . . . this is what *real* angels do? Did the nurses and staff members at the nursing home know they were angels in my life the day my dad passed away? Their tender words and kind acts consoled me more than I can say. Did David know that when he stayed with me constantly that difficult day that he was being an angel in my life? His arms placed around me when I felt my heart was breaking showed his love for me. Did my mother know she was a special angel in my life by making sure I had a wonderful childhood and that every Christmas held a treasure chest of memories all its own? I'm not sure angels always know who they are, but I do believe with all my heart that they are sent into our lives to help us as we journey along our earthly path. Whether they are family or friends, we need to be looking for them, and when we find them we need to cherish them.

Thank you to the many angels who have walked in and out of my life . . . and especially to those who chose to stay. Allow me to walk in your footsteps . . . the footsteps of earth's angels.

Betty Van Orden, Author

On earth, angels' wings are on the inside.

Author Unknown

Chapter Two

Follow the Savior

It's never too late to become what you might have been.

George Eliot

We pondered and prayed about what our theme should be for this year and what gifts we could give to bring the theme into the lives of our family during the holiday season. When considering all that our country is experiencing at this time, we decided our theme would be *Follow the Savior*. We have been counseled by many leaders that if we will follow our Savior and His teachings, we will find our greatest source of light, support, and peace. When tempted to make a wrong choice or to neglect doing something for someone who may need our help, we should stop and remember the example of our Savior. He was always kind to everyone and served them through His good works. This year, we will encourage our family to look beyond themselves and search for ways to become more like our Savior. We want our family to help others more willingly, forgive more readily, look for ways to make others happy, and show gratitude more often. May our gifts to Him and to others be as selfless as was His gift to us.

Never did the Savior give in expectation. I know of no case in His life in which there was an exchange. He was always the giver, seldom the recipient. Never did He give shoes, hose or a vehicle; never did He give perfume, a shirt or a fur wrap. His gifts were of such a nature that the recipient could hardly exchange or return the value. His gifts were rare ones; eyes to the blind, ears to the deaf and legs to the lame; cleanliness to the unclean, wholeness to the infirm and breath to the lifeless. His friends gave Him shelter food and love. He gave them of Himself, His love, His service, His life. He gave them and all their fellow mortals resurrection, salvation and eternal life.

Spencer W. Kimball,
The Church of Jesus Christ of Latter-day Saints

On the FIRST Day of

Christmas

We bring to you with love . . .

Story of the Meaning of Christmas! As you read the following story together, take turns reaching into the bag to bring out the gifts. This is a beautiful story, and we know you are going to love it. Find a special place to put your little tree after you have it decorated and, hopefully, it will serve as a reminder of the true meaning of Christmas.

✳ ✳ ✳ ✳ ✳

I made a bag out of velveteen and placed each of the items from the story inside the bag. I tied the bag with gold cord and it looked great. Each of the items was easy to find by shopping in craft stores. Some of them were purchased in the section that sells small wooden ornaments that can be painted. You can choose from a variety of ornaments. Sterling and I had some great evenings together painting the ornaments. You can also find finished ornaments that are ready to use.

The Meaning of Christmas

Just a week before Christmas I had a visitor. This is how it happened. I had just finished the household chores for the night and was preparing to go to bed when I heard a noise in the front of the house. I opened the door to the front room, and to my surprise, Santa himself stepped out from behind the Christmas tree. He placed his finger over his mouth so I would not cry out. "What are you doing?" I started to ask him.

The words choked in my throat, as I saw he had tears in his eyes. His usual jolly manner was gone. Gone was the eager boisterous soul we all know. He then answered me with a simple statement, "Teach the children!" I was puzzled. What did he mean? He anticipated my questions, and with one quick movement brought forth a miniature toy bag from behind the tree.

As I stood there bewildered, Santa said, "Teach the children! Teach them the old meaning of Christmas. The meaning that a now-a-day Christmas has forgotten!"

Santa then reached in his bag and pulled out a FIR TREE and placed it on the mantle. "Teach the children that the pure green color of the stately fir tree remains green all year round, depicting the everlasting hope of mankind. All the needles point heavenward, making it a symbol of man's thoughts turning toward heaven."

He again reached into his bag and pulled out a brilliant STAR. "Teach the children that the star was the heavenly sign of promises long ago. God promised a Savior for the world, and the star was the sign of fulfillment of that promise."

He then reached into the bag and pulled out a CANDLE. "Teach the children that the candle symbolizes that Christ is the light of the world, and when we see this great light we are reminded of Him who displaces the darkness."

Once again he reached into his bag and then removed a WREATH and placed it on the tree. "Teach the children that the wreath symbolizes the eternal nature of love. Real love never ceases. Love is one continuous round of affection."

He then pulled out from his bag an ornament of HIMSELF. "Teach the children that Santa Clause symbolizes the generosity and good will we feel during the month of December."

He reached in again and pulled out a HOLLY LEAF. "Teach the children that the holly plant represents immortality. It represents the crown of thorns worn by our Savior. The red holly berries represent blood shed by Him."

Next he pulled out a GIFT from the bag and said, "Teach the children that God so loved the world that He gave His only begotten Son. Thanks be to God for His unspeakable gift. Teach the children that the wise men bowed before the holy babe and presented Him with gold, frankincense, and myrrh. We should give gifts in the same spirit as the wise men."

Santa then reached in his bag and pulled out a CANDY CANE and hung it on the tree. "Teach the children that the candy cane represents the shepherd's crook. The crook on the shepherd's staff helps bring back strayed sheep from the flock. The candy cane is the symbol that we are our brother's keeper."

He reached in again and pulled out an ANGEL. "Teach the children that it was the angels that heralded the glorious news of the Savior's birth. The angels sang 'Glory to God in the highest, on earth, peace and good will.'"

Suddenly I heard a soft tinkling sound, and from his bag he pulled out a BELL. "Teach the children that as the lost sheep are found by the sound of a bell, it should bring people to the fold. The bell symbolizes guidance and return."

Santa looked at the tree and was pleased. He looked back at me and I saw the twinkle was back in his eyes. He said, "Remember, teach the children the true meaning of Christmas, and not to put me in the center, for I am but a humble servant of the One who is, and I bow down and worship Him, our Lord, our God."

Author Unknown

On the SECOND Day of

Christmas

We bring to you with love . . .

A Porcelain Statue of Christ Holding a Lamb! This statue of Jesus is especially beautiful and has great meaning to us. It teaches us about the "Good Shepherd." Some very dear friends of ours at the Conference Center presented us with a statue like this, and we love it so much and want you to have one also. Read the following story together and think of the Good Shepherd and of His love for each one of us.

These statues can be found in most Christian bookstores. They come in wonderful heavy-duty boxes for mailing. We felt sure this beautiful statue was going to be cherished for years to come.

In a talk given by Elder John R. Lasater in 1988, he explains the meaning of a "Good Shepherd." He said that years earlier he'd had the privilege of visiting Morocco as part of an official United States government delegation. As he traveled through the countryside in a group of five large black limousines, he noticed that the limousine in front of them was pulled off to the side of the road where he sensed an accident had occurred. He said that what he saw in the next few minutes has remained with him for many years. This is his story:

> An old shepherd, in the long, flowing robes of the Savior's day, was standing near the limousine in conversation with the driver nearby. I

noted a small flock of sheep numbering not more than fifteen or twenty. An accident had occurred. The king's vehicle had struck and injured one of the sheep belonging to the old shepherd. The driver of the vehicle was explaining to him the law of the land. Because the king's vehicle has injured one of the sheep belonging to the old shepherd, he was now entitled to one hundred times its value at maturity. However, under the same law, the injured sheep must be slain and the meat divided among the people. My interpreter hastily added, "But the old shepherd will not accept the money. They never do."

Startled, I asked him, "Why?" And he said, "Because of the love he has for each of his sheep." It was then that I noticed the old shepherd reach down, lift the injured lamb in his arms, and place it in a large pouch on the front of his robe. He kept stroking its head, repeating the same word over and over again. When I asked the meaning of the word, I was informed, "Oh, he is calling it by name. All of his sheep have a name, for he is their shepherd, and the good shepherds know each one of their sheep by name."

It was as my driver predicted. The money was refused, and the old shepherd with his small flock of sheep, with the injured one tucked safely in the pouch on his robe, disappeared into the beautiful desert of Morocco (John R. Lasater, "Shepherds of Israel," *Ensign*, May 1988, 74–75).

May each of us be reminded of the love our Master has for us, for He is the Good Shepherd and we are His sheep. Each time you look at this beautiful statue, think how much you are loved by your family and especially by the Good Shepherd.

On the THIRD Day of

Christmas

We bring to you with love . . .

A Hand-embroidered Pillow! NeNa has spent many hours embroidering this pillow for you. As you read the words embroidered on your pillow, you will be reminded of the counsel to "Follow the Savior." We also hope you will enjoy the enclosed story. Some of your favorite candy is included, so eat up!

❄ ❄ ❄ ❄ ❄

Patterns and instructions for embroidering pillows can easily be found in any store that sells fabric. You might choose to make your own design if you don't find exactly what you like. You could sketch a saying onto muslin fabric and embroider it. This can make your gift very personal and meaningful. Or choose a beautiful embroidered pillow already made. Make this work for you!

God's Embroidery

When I was little, my mother used to embroider a great deal. I would sit at her knee and look up from the floor and ask what she was doing. She informed me that she was embroidering. As from the underside, I watched her work within the boundaries of the little round hoop that she held in her hand. I complained to her that it sure looked messy from where I sat. She would smile at me, look down, and gently say, "My son, you go about your playing for a while, and when I am finished with my embroidering, I will put you on my knee and let you see it from my side." I wondered why she was using some dark threads along with the bright ones and why they seemed so jumbled from my view. A few minutes would pass and then I would hear Mother's voice say, "Son, come and sit on my knee." This I did only to be surprised and thrilled to see a beautiful flower or a sunset. I could not believe it.

Then Mother would say to me, "My son, from underneath it did look messy and jumbled, but you did not realize there was a pre-drawn plan on the top. It was a design. I was only following it. Now look at it from my side and you will see what I was doing."

Many times through the years I have looked up to my Heavenly Father and said, "Father, what are you doing?" He has answered, "I am embroidering your life." I say, "But it looks like a mess to me. It seems so jumbled. The threads seem so dark. Why can't they all be bright?"

The Father seems to tell me, "My child, you go about your business of doing my business, and one day I will bring you to Heaven and put you on my knee and you will see the plan from my side."

Anonymous

On the FOURTH Day of
Christmas
We bring to you with love . . .

New Christmas Books and Bookmarks! We hope you will enjoy the books we chose for you and that you will cuddle under your Christmas quilt and read the books together as a family. NeNa and PaPa made the beaded bookmarkers for you. They can be used throughout the year when you are reading either your library books or your scriptures. We are happy that you enjoy reading.

❉ ❉ ❉ ❉ ❉

My sister-in-law Susan brought these bookmarks to a family reunion and taught all the women how to make them. There were gorgeous beads from which to choose, and right away I knew this would be something our family would appreciate. Sterling and I made one for each member of our family with the hope that it would encourage them to read often and to enjoy it. Following are instructions for making the bookmarkers. They really are a great keepsake. The Christmas quilt I made for each family the first year we presented them with the 12 Days of Christmas is still being used. They love gathering under their quilt to read Christmas books and talk about their memories of Christmas past.

Instructions for Beaded Bookmarks

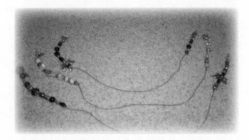

* Cut an 18 inch length of hemp cord.
* Make sure the beads you choose have holes big enough to fit over the hemp cord.
* Place the first knot about 3 inches up from one of the ends.
* Bead the end of the cord for about 1½ inches in the pattern you like.

Place a knot at the end of the beads to prevent them from moving.

* Measure from the top of your beads to the other side of the cord and make a knot 10 inches away. This will allow you 10 inches between the two sets of beads.

* Bead about 3 inches of beads on this end. It will be considered the bottom of the bookmarker.

* Knot off when you have put your beads on.

* Trim the ends of the cord to ¼ inch away from knot on both sides.

On the FIFTH Day of

Christmas
We bring to you with love . . .

A Day of Service! Today we would like for you to perform an act of service for someone. We are giving you some new baking pans to use in baking fresh Orange Nut Bread or any other bread you choose. So put on some Christmas music, heat up the oven, and make some delicious bread. Children, you will have such fun baking with Mom. When you are finished with your baking, we hope you will share some bread with your neighbors and friends. They will love you for it! We love you too!

❄ ❄ ❄ ❄ ❄

We knew our family would love new baking pans so we shopped at some of the kitchen specialty shops and found exactly what we were looking for. These pans can also be found at discount stores, as well. We included the recipe for the bread.

Orange Nut Bread
1 medium orange
1 cup raisins or dates
2 Tbsp. melted butter
1 tsp. vanilla
1 cup sugar

1 cup chopped nuts (optional)

1 egg, beaten

2 cups flour

½ tsp. salt

1 tsp. baking powder

½ tsp. baking soda

Wash orange; squeeze juice. Pour juice into a measuring cup and fill with boiling water to the 1 cup mark. Put orange rind and raisins through chopper (raisins may be left whole, if desired). Combine butter, sugar, vanilla, egg, and juice-water mixture. Mix well. Pour onto chopped fruits. Sift dry ingredients together and add to fruit mixture. Stir in nuts. Pour into well-greased 8x4x3 inch loaf pan. Bake 1 hour at 350 degrees.

On the SIXTH Day of

Christmas

We bring to you with love . . .

Mom's Night Off! This evening Papa and NeNa will arrive at your home with a pot of soup and some freshly baked bread. Mom doesn't have to worry about dinner tonight! We are including some darling soup bowls. Give Mom some extra kisses and let her know how much you love her. Oh, and perhaps you little ones can help set the table with your new soup bowls. Mom will love that! We love you so much!

✳ ✳ ✳ ✳ ✳

If you are mailing your gifts, you can send a recipe for soup and bread along with the soup bowls. Also, in some of the kitchen shops you can find pretty jars filled with ingredients for making soup. All that's needed is to empty the ingredients into a pot, add water and cook. They will have fresh soup in no time! That would be a wonderful gift to receive.

Italian Soup

Brown 1 lb. Italian Sausage

Sauté 1 cup chopped onion and 2 cloves garlic

Add 6 cups water and 2 cups chopped tomatoes; 5 beef bouillon cubes;
8-oz. can tomato sauce; 1 cup carrots; ½ tsp. oregano; ½ tsp. sweet
basil

Simmer uncovered for 30 minutes.

Add ½ cup chopped zucchini, 8 oz. tortellini, ¼ cup green pepper,
1 Tbsp. dry parsley

Simmer covered for 30 to 40 minutes.

On the SEVENTH Day of

Christmas

We bring to you with love . . .

A New Ornament for Your Memory Tree! This year we are giving
you a beautiful new ornament with red vinyl letters reading, "Follow the
Savior." As your memory tree fills with ornaments through the years, we
hope this year will be a special memory. May we ever be reminded of the
importance of following our Savior's example.

*I can always find these glass ornaments in any craft store, and they come in
various sizes. Vinyl lettering has become very popular so it shouldn't be difficult
to find. It's easy to put the vinyl on the glass balls. You can also purchase the vinyl
words in packages in most craft stores. I made a hanger for the ornament by tying
a pretty black and white polka dot ribbon through the top of the ornament. If you
can't find the vinyl lettering, you can always paint the letters on the ornament.
Puffy paint gives a great look.*

On the EIGHTH Day of
Christmas
We bring to you with love . . .

A New Game and Popcorn! We know how your family loves playing games, so today you are receiving a great new one called Phase 10. Also, we are including a game for the younger children. It's called Shrek Operation, and it's so much fun to play. Watch out because we are going to give you lots of competition! Make some popcorn (which we have included) and enjoy an evening together. There is nothing more special than spending time together as a family. What a great way to follow the Savior. We will be thinking of you!

✳ ✳ ✳ ✳ ✳

We try to watch the advertisements during the holidays to see which games are the most popular for the year. Then we determine which games will be appropriate for the ages of the children. Playing games together and making wonderful memories is a priority with each family.

On the NINTH Day of
Christmas
We bring to you with love . . .

A Special Treat! Tonight you can have fun sharing this yummy treat. We have made this recipe during the years, and it has become one of our family favorites. Perhaps you can spend time talking about some of your special memories from the past while you eat your treat. Each one of you makes our memories wonderful!

✳ ✳ ✳ ✳ ✳

These recipes are easy and can be put in a pretty tin or glass container for gift giving. They are also easy to mail.

Sweet Corn Pops

1 cup butter

1 cup sugar

¼ cup water

Corn Pops

Using a large nonstick frying pan, melt the butter and sugar, and then add the water. Cook on high heat, letting it bubble. Stir constantly until it starts to turn a nice caramel color. You may add cashews or any other nuts you like at this point. Next, pour over a bowl of Corn Pops. Let cool. This recipe can also be poured out on a marble slab and makes a delicious brittle by not using the corn pops.

Peanut Brittle

1 cup white corn syrup

½ cup water

2 cups sugar

2 cups raw Spanish peanuts

½ tsp. butter

1 ½ tsp. salt

1½ tsp. vanilla

2 tsp. soda

Cook syrup, water, and sugar to soft ball stage. Add peanuts to the cooking mixture. Stir constantly until syrup turns a dark golden color. Remove from heat. Add butter, salt, vanilla, and soda. Stir. Pour mixture onto greased cookie sheet. After the mixture hardens, break into pieces.

On the TENTH Day of

Christmas

We bring to you with love . . .

A Silver Dollar! Some of you probably have never seen a silver dollar. They aren't in circulation as much as they were some years ago. I remember when

I was a little girl, I would receive a silver dollar for my birthday each year and sometimes a relative would give me another one for Christmas. I kept these among my most treasured gifts. Today I want to share some of them with you. When I read this little story I knew it was exactly how I wanted to use my silver dollars. I have put one for your family inside this shadow box so it will be protected. The easel will display your shadow box nicely. Read the following story together and make this a special memory for you. It makes us feel good to bring happiness to someone else. We never want to be the cause of another person being sad or unhappy.

Silver dollars may be difficult to find, but a fifty cent piece would also be exciting to give. You might use some money you have saved or collected that you now want to share with your family. I found small black-framed shadow boxes to put the silver dollars in so they would be protected. Shadow boxes are also found at most craft stores.

Far away in a small village, two young boys were strolling through the fields on their way to the market. There were many villagers working out in the fields. As they were walking, they came across a pair of shoes sitting at the end of a row. The younger boy said to his older brother in an excited voice, "Let's hide these shoes and when the owner comes out of the field, we can watch him look and wonder where his shoes are. It will be great fun to tease this person." The older brother said to the boy, "These shoes mean a lot to this worker. He cares so much for his shoes that he left them here so they wouldn't get ruined. Why don't we give him a better surprise than thinking he has lost his prized shoes. We will put a silver dollar in each shoe and then we will hide and watch his delight when he finds the treasure in his shoes. It is much better to give happiness to someone than to cause them pain or distress." The young boy learned a great lesson that day as he watched the field worker find his surprise. He was happy inside as he watched the man smile and look around in wonder. He realized just how good it made him feel to bring joy and happiness to someone else.

AUTHOR UNKNOWN

On the ELEVENTH Day of

Christmas

We bring to you with love . . .

A Beautiful Picture of the Savior! Since our theme for this year has been "Follow the Savior," we thought it would be especially nice for each family to have a new picture of Christ to hang in your homes. Try to always remember that our Savior desires us to *see ourselves as He sees us.* He knows our capabilities and what we can become. May we each be touched by His love and always do our best as we follow Him.

❄ ❄ ❄ ❄ ❄

We can never have too many reminders of our need to always live the best we can. There were lots of pictures from which we could choose. Again, this can be mailed if your family lives away.

On the TWELFTH Day of

Christmas

We bring to you with love . . .

A Leather Camel! Papa found these camels on the Internet, and we were thrilled with them. We felt this would be the perfect way to conclude our 12 Days of Christmas this year. Again, we have a wonderful story to share with you. It was written and shared with us by a sweet lady from Aberdeen, Idaho. As we "Follow the Savior," we will be reminded of the importance of prayer and knowing that He desires to help us throughout our lives. He is always there for us and He loves us. We want you to know that we love each one of you with all our hearts. Always know we desire for you to continue to "Follow the Savior."

❄ ❄ ❄ ❄ ❄

The camel truly was the perfect conclusion to our 12 Days of Christmas! The message said exactly what we desired to leave in the hearts of our family members. The Internet is a good place to find camels and there is usually a nice variety from which to choose. The ones we liked best are made of leather, but there were many just as nice. Start looking for these early since there will be shipping involved and that can be risky during the holidays.

The Secret of the Camel

The camel is an interesting animal. It is not one of the most beautiful. It has thick matted hair that falls off in clumps. It has knobby knees and a big hump on its back. It is referred to as a ruminant because it regurgitates its swallowed food to chew again, and then swallows it again. However, the camel is a wonderful pack animal. It is used for transportation in many countries. Camels can carry up to six hundred pounds and average twenty miles a day over rugged terrain. They can travel in hot conditions and go for long periods of time without water. They truly are amazing animals. Regardless of its looks or mannerisms, a camel is loved by its master, for it is useful, obedient, and needed.

Here is the camel's secret. . . . Each night, at the end of a long day, the camel kneels at the feet of his master. His master carefully lifts the burden from the camel's back so it can rest comfortably through the night. The next morning, the camel kneels again before his master, and the master gently places the burden on the camel's back for another day. He is careful to re-arrange things here or there if he sees that the pack is wearing a sore spot. This enables the camel to carry his burden for another day.

At Christmas, we celebrate the birth of our Savior, Jesus Christ. Throughout His life, the Savior was referred to as Master. He loves us regardless of our looks or mannerisms. He desires for us to be useful and obedient. May we practice the secret of the camel. As we kneel each night at the feet of our Master, may He lift our burdens, that we may rest well and comfortably. As we kneel each morning, may we realize that He knows of our pain, our suffering, and our sorrows, for He has felt them all. May our faith in the Lord Jesus Christ be sufficient to help us carry our burdens . . . for just one more day.

REBECCA PULLIAM, ABERDEEN, IDAHO

It is a time to do what is right regardless of the consequences that might follow. . . . We have nothing to fear. God is at the helm. He will overrule for the good of His work.

GORDON B. HINCKLEY

Chapter Three

Christmas Traditions

Like snowflakes, my Christmas memories gather and dance—each
beautiful, unique, and too soon gone.

DEBORAH SHIPP

Renee Wolf and I have become great friends since we visit together each
month. She has a real flair for decorating, and her home shows her talents.
As we were visiting together one October day, I shared with Renee my plans
for the 12 Days of Christmas that year. She liked my ideas and shared with
me her desire to present the 12 Days of Christmas for her family also. She
could tell from my excitement that it, indeed, brings great joy to the giver as
well as the receiver. We spent an hour or more sharing ideas and suggestions
of things we felt would be fun and exciting for each of our families.

When I returned to visit Renee in November, she had a complete plan
of what she was doing for her family, and it was terrific. I asked her if she
would allow me to share some of her ideas with you in this book. Being the
outstanding mother, grandmother, and friend that she is, she quickly gave
her consent and offered me copies of some of the things she was planning.
As we go through this year, you will see why it was so exciting. With her
permission, I have added a few thoughts and ideas of my own along the
way.

On the FIRST Day of
Christmas
We bring to you with love . . .

"BELIEVE" Blocks! A tradition in our family is to discuss our belief of the true meaning of Christmas. Maybe we should have Christmas traditions all year round. You see, at Christmastime most people change for the better. Is it because of the great yuletide carols, the festive atmosphere everywhere you go, or just some hidden part in all of us that screams out "*I believe in more than what I see around me*"? Somewhere inside, we all believe in something better than we now have or see. Most of us feel a lot better when we help someone. This is what we call the *feeling* of Christmas, and we should strive to feel this way all year long. These blocks can be placed on a shelf where they can be seen and enjoyed by everyone.

❄ ❄ ❄ ❄ ❄

I found these darling red, wooden blocks while shopping at a nearby boutique. The letters spelling "Believe" were painted in black. Since then I have seen them at many craft stores. If you are handy with a saw and sander, you could make the blocks any size you want, sand them until they are smooth, and paint them any color you choose. You can use the vinyl letters that are popular now or you could paint the letters on them. It would definitely be a nice keepsake from you to them. There is something wonderful about having someone make a gift just for you.

On the SECOND Day of
Christmas
We bring to you with love . . .

A Flannel Board and a Story of the Nativity! As far back as I can remember, we always had a flannel board in our home with many wonderful stories we learned by using it. This was always one of my favorite traditions. Today you are receiving your own flannel board with pieces of the nativity so you can teach your children about the greatest gift ever given to mankind. Without this gift there would be no "Reason for the Season."

❋ ❋ ❋ ❋ ❋

These pieces can be found online, or you may choose to get them from a coloring book. Cut them out and glue a piece of flannel to the back of each piece. This allows them to stick to the flannel on the flannel board. A flannel board can easily be made by covering a piece of hardboard with flannel. Framing the flannel board will give it a more finished look. This will be a fun activity and another way of teaching the importance for each one of us to remember the birth of our Savior.

The pieces to the story can be placed in the following order:

1. Stable	11. Star
2. Palm tree	12. Angel
3. Bird	13. Angel
4. Nest	14. Shepherd Man
5. Big Sheep	15. Shepherd Boy
6. Lamb	16. Camel
7. Donkey	17. Wiseman
8. Joseph	18. Wiseman
9. Mary	19. Wiseman
10. Manger	20. Baby Jesus

On the THIRD Day of

Christmas

We bring to you with love . . .

New Christmas Stockings! Legend has it that the tradition of hanging Christmas stockings by the fireplace began with two poor sisters. Both wanted to marry, but their father was too poor to pay for their wedding dowries. One Christmas Eve, the sisters hung their stockings by the fire to dry. Saint Nicholas intervened, tossing gold coins down the chimney and into the sisters' stockings. On Christmas Day, the sisters were delighted to discover the money—enough for both of their dowries. Victorian children sometimes hung their Christmas stockings on their bedposts. The story goes that parents during that time had a recipe for stocking gift-giving that still works today.

> "Something to eat, something to read,
> Something to play with, and something they need."

Our family waited until Christmas Eve to hang our Christmas stocking by the fireplace. The children in our family hung the typical store-bought red ones with white fur on top. Mom and Dad usually borrowed stockings from Dad's sock drawer. Our stockings were always full of fun surprises and candy, typically things we hadn't even asked Santa to bring. Santa always put an orange in the toe, that was a given!

Every year Dad found a lump of coal in the bottom of his stocking. Santa was letting him know that he needed to be a good boy next year. Traditionally, Santa leaves one lump of coal to remind mischievous children to be good. However, if you are really naughty, a lump of coal is all you will get in your stocking. One Christmas, Dad's stocking was found empty with the exception of one single lump of coal. My heart was broken! How could Santa have thought my Dad was such a bad boy. That night I wrote a letter to Santa asking why he had given my dad something I thought he didn't deserve. I cried and cried. Dad tried to console me but I was too heartbroken. The only solution I could come up with was to share some of my goodies with him to make him feel better. That was the last Christmas Santa left coal in Dad's stocking. I guess Dad and Santa learned a valuable lesson. Always remember, "You better watch out, you better not cry, you better not pout, I'm telling you why; Santa Claus is coming to town."

Hanging our stockings was truly a favorite tradition in our home. These new stockings were made especially for you and will hold lots of treats from Santa, so hang them where he will be sure to see them.

❄ ❄ ❄ ❄ ❄

There are many stockings in the stores, from elaborate to sport themes to Disney. If you don't find exactly what you're looking for, then you may want to consider making stockings. Patterns for stockings are found in just about every fabric store. It's fun to personalize stockings so family members know which stocking is just for them! The lumps of coal can be found in many of the stores during the holidays as candy rather than coal. It's made to look like a lump of coal and is a fun treat for the children.

On the FOURTH Day of
Christmas
We bring to you with love . . .

New Christmas Place Mats and Napkins! It's no secret that one of my favorite things about Christmas is adorning our home with all the traditional holiday decorations. I usually dread the task, but once it's done, I love the sensation that comes over me. Our home somehow seems to transport me back in time in my heart . . . the time spent with family. I reflect on many of the Christmas holidays spent with relatives and on how blessed I am to be a part of such a loving family. I feel a sense of peace and serenity when I sit quietly by the Christmas tree. I begin to think about how grateful I am that I have been blessed with all the necessities and comforts of life. I cherish the family gatherings that come with the season and hope we can continue to be close to one another. We hope you enjoy today's gift of new place mats for your table. We love making pretty things for you and sharing our traditions with those we love!

The huge sales after Thanksgiving are a great time to shop for new place mats. The prices are great and the selection is usually good. You could shop for some fabric that matches the décor of each family and have fun making place mats for them. This way you can make them exactly the way you like and you won't have to worry about finding the exact number you need . . . you can make plenty for each family.

On the FIFTH Day of
Christmas
We bring to you with love . . .

A Santa Plate and Coloring Book! Enjoy coloring a picture for Santa from your new coloring book. On Christmas Eve leave the picture along with some yummy cookies on your new Santa plate. Santa will love seeing that you have a special plate just for him, and he will cherish the wonderful picture you have colored.

❊　❊　❊　❊　❊

Leaving cookies for Santa was always a tradition in my home as a little girl and it continued with our children after I was married. Santa plates can easily be found. I've seen them in many shapes and colors, and they really do make it fun for the children to have a special plate on which to leave cookies for Santa.

Dear Santa

Snowflakes softly falling
upon your window they play,
Your blankets snug around you
into sleep you drift away.
I bend to gently kiss you
when I see that on the floor.
There's a letter neatly written,
I wonder who it's for.
I quietly unfold it,
making sure you're still asleep
It's a Christmas list for Santa,
one my heart will always keep.
It started just as always
with the toys seen on TV
A new watch for your father
and a winter coat for me.
But as my eyes read on
I could see that deep inside
There were many things you wished for
that your loving heart would hide.
You asked if your friend Molly
could have another Dad.
It seems her father hits her,
and it makes you very sad.
Then you asked dear Santa,
if the neighbors down the street

could find a job, that they might have
some food, and clothes, and heat?
You saw a family on the news
whose house had blown away
"Dear Santa, send them just one thing
a place where they can stay.
And Santa, those four cookies that
I left you for a treat
could you take them to the children
who have nothing else to eat?
Do you know that bear I have,
the one I love so dear?
I'm leaving it for you to take
to Africa this year.
And as you fly your reindeer
on this night of Jesus' birth
Could your magic bring to everyone
goodwill and peace on earth?
There's one last thing before you go
so grateful I would be
If you'd smile at Baby Jesus
in the manger by our tree."
I pulled the letter close to me
I felt it melt my heart,
those tiny hands had written
what no other could impart.
"And a little child shall lead them"
was whispered in my ear
As I watched you sleep on Christmas Eve
while Santa Claus was here.

AUTHOR UNKNOWN

On the SIXTH Day of
Christmas
We bring to you with love . . .

An Evening of Sharing Family Traditions! What a fun evening we have planned for you tonight. We will all meet at NeNa and PaPa's house at seven o'clock. We are going to share with you some stories of traditions that we had in our families when we were children. We're also asking the parents in each family to come prepared to share one tradition they can recall while they were growing up in their homes. It could be a certain food that was prepared as a tradition at Christmastime. Hey, how about bringing us a sample! The grandchildren will love hearing these stories and, hopefully, they will recognize that you still do some of these traditions in their homes today. Traditions are wonderful and are great reminders of our heritage. We are grateful for the traditions we cherish from our childhood. Let us share some of these with you tonight and while you listen to our stories, we will have lots of treats for you to enjoy. Many of these have become traditions in our family. We can hardly wait to see you and give you big hugs!

❄ ❄ ❄ ❄ ❄

If your family lives away, you could write stories of the traditions you have. Invite the family to gather around the tree and have Mom or Dad read these stories. You could even mail some treats that have become traditions. If you can't mail them, then perhaps you could send the recipes. Children love hearing stories of when we were young like them. This is a beautiful way to share our lives with them and especially our Christmas traditions.

On the SEVENTH Day of

Christmas

We bring to you with love . . .

Musical Instruments for your family! My friend Renee shared the following story with me: Probably my most favorite tradition in our family as a young girl was playing and singing Christmas carols. My mother made sure everyone learned the art of music. We were all coached in voice, piano, and playing instruments. A perfect evening would be when all our family gathered together with the instruments we had learned to play and each one of us would play the very best we could to show our gratitude to Mother for inspiring us. There were times when we chose to just sing and enjoy the words to the carols together. I loved these evenings! Even today, my heart becomes very full with these memories. Music has always had an emotional effect on me. It can cheer me up, relax me, and even inspire me to be a better person. I truly believe Christmas would not seem like Christmas without the singing of carols and the sounds of the instruments. We hope you will enjoy your musical instrument and Christmas song book. My dad and my grandfather played the harmonica and were quite good at it. This year we have purchased a harmonica for each family. We have included toy musical instruments for the children. Please practice between now and our family Christmas Eve party, so we can all play together from your new song book.

❄ ❄ ❄ ❄ ❄

You can find lots of inexpensive instruments for your family to begin playing. If you want to invest in an instrument for the adults to play, you can visit a music store and see what they have to offer. It might be wise to see how seriously they take your idea of playing a musical instrument before investing too much money. But it can be such fun.

On the EIGHTH Day of

Christmas

We bring to you with love . . .

A Day of Baking with Grandma! Another of our family traditions was baking sugar cookies with Mother. I remember making star, tree, snowman, stocking, and angel-shaped cookies. Mother always let me help decorate the cookies with lots of sprinkles and several colors of icing. This was one of the traditions that truly made Christmas seem like Christmas. The smell of the cookies baking is one I shall never forget. Today you are coming to our home so we can bake together and make wonderful memories. Grandmothers love baking with their grandchildren and hold tight to such precious opportunities. I have some new recipes we will make, and you will be the testers to see just how good they really are. Perhaps when we have finished, we will deliver cookies to some of our neighbors. They will love that!

❄ ❄ ❄ ❄ ❄

There is nothing quite as special as baking cookies with grandchildren. I made sure I had lots of decorations and plenty of colors of icing for the cookies. It was fun putting together many of my favorite recipes for a small cookbook for each grandchild. The grandchildren loved having their very own cookbook, and this made a nice keepsake for them. This makes a wonderful gift for mailing, and one they can use throughout the entire year.

Sugar Cookies

1 cup softened butter

2 cups sugar

3 eggs

1 tsp. vanilla

1 cup sour cream

6 cups flour

1 tsp. salt

2 tsp. soda

¼ tsp. nutmeg

Cream together butter, sugar, eggs and vanilla. Stir in sour cream. Mix dry ingredients together and add flour. Mix all together well. Refrigerate dough for 2 hours. Roll out and cut to approximately ¼ in. thickness. Bake at 350 degrees for 5 to 8 minutes.

Frosting

2 cups powdered sugar

½ stick butter

2 to 3 Tbsp. evaporated milk

1 tsp. vanilla

Beat all together until smooth. Use food coloring for tinting.

On the NINTH Day of

Christmas

We bring to you with love . . .

New Hats and Gloves! Spending time with our family has always been a favorite tradition for us. In 1970, Monday night was designated as Family Night in our church. Many other people have decided to follow this weekly habit in their families. We are encouraged to give highest priority to this special night. We have been promised that our dedication to this program will help protect our families against the evils of our time and will bring us abundant joy now and throughout the eternities. We hope you will reserve a night each week to bring your family together for instruction and fun. Tonight, being Family Night, we will visit the city and enjoy the beautiful lights and the nativity. Put on your new hat and gloves so you will be warm. We look forward to spending an evening with you. Perhaps we should stop for some hot chocolate on the way home. How does that sound? Can't wait to see you!

❄ ❄ ❄ ❄ ❄

Finding cute hats and gloves wasn't difficult at all. You should be able to find them in any of your local discount stores. We found ones especially for the holiday, and the grandchildren love them. We took lots of pictures since they looked absolutely adorable.

On the TENTH Day of
Christmas
We bring to you with love . . .

A New Photo Album! Each year during Christmas, our family would spend at least one evening going through our picture albums. These albums had been filled with pictures taken during Christmas in years past. The albums were always full to overflowing with wonderful memories. What a fun tradition this became in our family. Today you are receiving your own Christmas photo album personalized with your name and the year. Before you know it, you will have collected many Christmas albums and, hopefully, this tradition will be passed on through generations for your family to enjoy.

❄ ❄ ❄ ❄ ❄

Any photo album can be used. You can either have it engraved or let them decide how they want to finish it. Make it as personable as you want it to be. This is sure to be one of the favorite gifts you give. Perhaps you could include a disposable camera to let the children take their own pictures and have them include some in their family Christmas album. Grandchildren love taking pictures.

On the ELEVENTH Day of

Christmas

We bring to you with love . . .

New Christmas Pillowcases! It's a fun tradition in our family during the holidays to switch our regular pillowcases to Christmas pillowcases . . . and this year NeNa has made new ones for each member of your family. There are different patterns and prints for each person. We think you are going to love them! So before you go to bed tonight, put your new pillowcase on your pillow. You are sure to have sweet dreams! Always remember how much we love you.

❄ ❄ ❄ ❄ ❄

What a fun project this turned out to be! I shopped for the best fabric I could possibly find for my family and got busy sewing pillowcases for them to use during the season. Each year the grandchildren will anxiously await the day they can replace their regular pillowcases with ones made especially for the holidays. It's such fun making something I know they will enjoy so much. I'm including the instructions for making the pillowcases and the cute little poem I included with them. The grandchildren loved it!

Pillowcase Poem

He's making a list and checking it twice
Going to find out who's naughty or nice,
I checked out the good names and what do you know?
Your name was missing! I hollered, "Oh, no!"
"Oh Santa," I pleaded, "Joe's not really bad!"
He's a pretty good kid. I'll vouch for the lad!"
So Santa relented. A gift you'll receive
If you whisper to Santa, of course, I believe.
Sweet dreams, Love, Grandma

Joyce Kay Goodrich, Author

Standard-size Pillowcases

* Cut 27 inches of fabric that is 45 inches wide. Cotton or flannel Christmas prints are great.
* Cut 9 inches of contrasting fabric; fold to 4½ inches wide and press.
* Cut a 4 inch piece of fabric—fold to 2 inches wide and press. Choose a color to highlight one of the colors from your main fabric.
* Layer 27-inch piece, then 2-inch piece and finally the 4½-inch piece.
* Sew through all three layers. This forms the casing and trim.
* Sew across the end and down one side.

On the TWELFTH Day of

Christmas

We bring to you with love . . .

Volunteering in a Homeless Shelter! A tender tradition in our family when I was a child was that of volunteering at a homeless shelter on Christmas Day. We would open our gifts from Santa and have a wonderful breakfast together. Then we would get dressed and drive to a local shelter where we would help cook for and feed the homeless. This was a humbling experience for our family. Today we want you to share this experience with us. Your lives will never be the same again. We have been told in the scriptures that as we serve those around us, we are in the service of our God. Today is a perfect day to be found in the service of our God. We look forward to sharing time with you.

❄ ❄ ❄ ❄ ❄

Check your directories for phone numbers and addresses for homeless shelters. Call and ask questions about what they need and the hours they will need help. This can be a memory for your family that they will never forget—a great act of service!

Chapter Four

Imagination

Probably the reason we all go so haywire at Christmastime with the endless unrestrained and often silly buying of gifts is that we don't quite know how to put our love into words.

HARLON MILLER

One of the most amazing and memorable themes we have used was the year we introduced the Christmas Elf to each family. Oh, what excitement! Each family was given an elf that had come directly from the North Pole to spend Christmas with them. We chose the same elf for each family so there wouldn't be a challenge as to who had the best elf. A tiny jar of "elf magic snowflakes" came with the elf, and the children were told to sprinkle some of the magic snowflakes on the elf each night before going to bed. This would allow their new little friend to come to life during the night. This thrilled the children beyond words. We thought it was wonderful that each family gave their elf a name, and he instantly became a member of their family. The younger grandchildren carried their new friend around with them all day and our granddaughter Brooke took him to "show-and-tell" at kindergarten. He was instantly loved!

Many mornings they awoke to find that the elf had gotten into quite a bit of trouble while they were sleeping. Our phone would be ringing or our email would be full of pictures and comments each morning as our grand-children reported the happenings of their elf the night before. One morning there was a picture of Daddy with the word "Willie" written across his forehead in lipstick and also some lipstick on his lips and other makeup on his face. Willie, the little elf, had gotten into Mom's makeup during the night and decorated Dad's face with it. They also included a picture of Dad as he looked in the mirror and saw what Willie had done to him while he was sleeping. Oh, the excitement of those sweet little children telling us what Willie had gotten into during the night. One family has four boys, so their elf, "Guido," got into the boys' underwear drawer and had put underwear all over the Christmas tree and the mantle. "Dexter" drove the family car one night to an all-night burger shop and had himself some great food. He left wrappers all over the car, while "Buddy" got in the refrigerator and somehow had turned the family's milk green! Buddy was sitting beside the milk, looking very innocent. "Eddie" managed to toilet-paper the girls' bathroom and even had some going down the hall. The girls laughed hysterically when they awoke to that! "Alex" loved the new baby in the home, so during the night he got in the baby's swing and spent the night there eating some cookies. He had left crumbs in the swing for Mommy to clean up. The elves weren't always mischievous. One morning one of the elves was found in the nativity holding the baby Jesus and feeding him a cracker. Another time he had set out the scriptures and had left a note for the family to join together and read the story of the birth of the Savior before going to bed. We found that these little elves might be a bit naughty at times, but they also wanted the children to remember the true meaning of Christmas.

The tales of these elves were priceless as we listened, oh so carefully, to each grandchild talking as fast as he or she could, hoping to be the first to tell their story. This truly was one of the most magical Christmases ever. Our children had made it such fun for their families as they knew this would delight us. Anticipating the results of introducing the elves to each of the families, we had decided to have our theme for that year to be *Imagination!* In today's world, we often lose the thrill of using our imaginations, but an imagination is such a wonderful gift that we never want to lose. We tried to adjust the gifts that year to the theme in some way. Some of the gifts were a little more difficult, but it all worked out, and our family loved it. They are still talking about their elves and can hardly wait until next Christmas when the elf has promised to return and spend another holiday with them.

On the FIRST Day of
Christmas
We bring to you with love . . .

Imagine . . . A New Friend! This little elf has come from the North Pole to spend the holidays with you. He begged Santa to let him visit with the hopes that you will grow to love him as much as he loves you. Your elf will need a name, so decide together as a family what his name is going to be. Each night you will sprinkle him with the magic elf snowflakes he has brought with him. If you do this, he will come to life during the night. We have heard that he can sometimes be very mischievous, so watch out! This little elf will be such fun for you and he will become a great friend. Enjoy him and use your *imagination* when you play with him.

❄ ❄ ❄ ❄ ❄

Sterling and I looked in many stores before finding the elf we thought would be perfect for our families. He had to have a happy face! It took a while but we found just the elf we wanted. You can also find wonderful elves on the Internet. Some of these elves come with ideas and suggestions of what the elf can do while the children are sleeping. This truly is lots of fun for both you and your family!

On the SECOND Day of
Christmas
We bring to you with love . . .

Imagine . . . going to "The Amazing Race"! Yes, you are coming to NeNa and PaPa's house tonight for The Amazing Race. We are going to have such a wonderful time together! Our evening will begin with pizza, salads, sodas, and dessert. Following dinner, we will begin The Amazing Race. You have been divided into teams, so check the enclosed list to see which team you will be on. There will be prizes and treats for everyone, so be at our home at 6:30 PM and we'll get started. Can you *imagine* an evening with more fun?

❄ ❄ ❄ ❄ ❄

This proved to be an incredible evening for both our children and the grand-children. The parents were busy snapping pictures throughout the evening. We had relay races of all kinds. One was to carry a Styrofoam ball (representing a snowball) on a spoon in your mouth across the room and empty it into a pail. Then you would hurry back and tag the next person in line so they could quickly do the same thing. The first team to finish, of course, was the winner.

A second relay was to put Vaseline on the cheeks, noses, and chins of the children. We had a bucket filled with cotton balls. They were to put their faces into the bucket and see how many cotton balls they could get to attach to their faces . . . making them look as though they had a Santa beard. Their hands had to be behind them! They loved this one! We counted the cotton balls and the team getting the most was the winner.

Another relay was to line up in teams. The first person in line races across the room to a table where they find a pair of gloves. They put on the gloves, unwrap a candy kiss, eat it, remove the gloves, and race back to tag the next person in line. That person follows the same instructions, until all players have gone. The first team to finish wins.

We had an adult stationed at each of the events to give a little help to those who were just too young to complete the task, but who definitely didn't want to be left out of the excitement. Think of more fun games for the children and, remember, they love competition!

Another relay they especially enjoyed was racing across the room to a stack of Christmas items which they had to put on, have their picture taken, take the items off again, and race back to tag the next person in line. They looked adorable and were laughing so hard they could hardly get the clothing on and off. We used such things as a Santa hat, socks, Christmas apron, and gloves. If you are mail-ing your 12 Days of Christmas, why not send some of the items with instructions on playing the relays and perhaps you could include a few prizes for everyone. Dollar stores are great places to buy inexpensive prizes. Everything would be easy to mail. The parents would love having such a fun evening with their children, especially when everything has been provided for them. You could send a coupon for pizza that Mom or Dad could pick up before the party begins. Since "you" are hosting the party, you might want to include some Christmas plates, napkins, and cups. You are sure to get lots of raves about this day's gift.

On the THIRD Day of

Christmas

We bring to you with love . . .

Imagine . . . your own copy of Mamma Mia! Do you remember how much fun we had with our "Girl's Night Out" and going to see this movie! Could we have been any happier! With memories like this, we wanted to make sure there was a copy in each of your homes, so each time you watch the DVD you will recall the fun we had together. Oh, to thank Dad for babysitting, we have included a gift certificate for a delicious hamburger and fries. Thanks for such wonderful memories!

❄ ❄ ❄ ❄ ❄

Any movie would be a great gift but if you have one that holds special memories, then maybe that's the one you want to give. DVDs are easy gifts to mail also.

On the FOURTH Day of

Christmas

We bring to you with love . . .

Imagine . . . lollipops to share with your best friend! Today you are to follow our yearly tradition and take a lollipop for you and one for your best friend. Friends are true treasures in our lives. They need to know how much you love them. Friends are one of God's most beautiful blessings to us.

❄ ❄ ❄ ❄ ❄

If you choose to make your lollipops, you'll find darling molds of all kinds in craft stores and in some discount stores. They usually carry the flavorings, sticks, and bags also. Some of our family favorites are blueberry, strawberry, cotton candy, and root beer. Again, this makes a gift that is easily mailed. Don't forget that lollipops of all shapes, sizes, and flavors are available to purchase in most discount stores and drugstores.

When you ask God for a gift . . . be thankful if He sends, not dia-
monds, pearls, or riches, but the love of real true friends.

HELEN STEINER RICE

 On the FIFTH Day of
Christmas
We bring to you with love . . .

Imagine . . . an "elf" ornament for your Christmas tree! Yes, this new ornament is for your tree that holds many memories throughout the years. This little elf will hang there to remind you of the first year your special elf came to stay with you during Christmas. Perhaps you will want to write his name on the back of the ornament. Isn't he adorable! You, too, are adorable! We love you.

❆ ❆ ❆ ❆ ❆

We found these darling little elf ornaments in a local department store. We
could hardly believe it when we found the elves and knew they were exactly the
ones we were hoping to find. If you plan your theme early in the year, you can
start looking for ornaments as soon as they are in the stores.

 On the SIXTH Day of
Christmas
We bring to you with love . . .

Imagine . . . your own Elf book! Gather round the tree tonight and read this fun little book about elves. It's a great story! Maybe you could have your own elf listen to the story with you. Oh, and we are including some tangerines for you to enjoy while you listen to Mom or Dad. Have fun and know how much we love you.

❆ ❆ ❆ ❆ ❆

Surprisingly, it wasn't difficult to find a storybook about elves. You might check the Internet if you don't find one in your local bookstores or library. This is also an easy gift to mail.

On the SEVENTH Day of

Christmas

We bring to you with love . . .

Imagine . . . a hat knitted just for you! Yes, NeNa has been very busy knitting these wonderful hats for each of you. Did you notice that your hats are in the colors of our Indian tribe? Be sure and bring your hats when we all go to the cabin after Christmas. You will look so adorable, and we will take lots of pictures. Hopefully, your hat will keep your ears nice and warm.

I bought knitting looms that made this project go a lot faster. After all, I did have thirty-two hats to knit! I had a lot of fun working on this project, knowing it was for our adorable children and grandchildren. Watch for the looms to go on sale or watch for a coupon and get them at a craft or fabric store. You'll find the yarn just about anywhere. The directions for knitting the hats come with the looms. In my first book, I told about the Indian tribe our family formed and that each family in the tribe has their own color. This made it even more fun since I used the color of yarn to match their tribal color. The children and grandchildren thought this was great.

The Plan of the Master Weaver

Our lives are but fine weavings
that God and we prepare,
Each life becomes a fabric planned
and fashioned in His care.
He may not always see just how
the weavings intertwine,
But we must trust the Master's hand
and follow His design.
For he can view the pattern
upon the upper side,
While we must look from underneath
and trust in Him to guide.
Sometimes a strand of sorrow
is added to His plan,
And though it's difficult for us
we still must understand.
That it's He who fills the shuttle
it's He who knows what's best,
So we must weave in patience
and leave to Him the rest.
Not till the loom is silent
and the shuttles cease to fly,
Shall God unroll the canvas
and explain the reason why.
The dark threads are as needed
in the Weaver's skillful hand,
As the threads of gold and silver
in the pattern He has planned.

AUTHOR UNKNOWN

On the EIGHTH Day of

Christmas

We bring to you with love . . .

Imagine . . . tickets to a Christmas concert! We're going to have a fabulous evening together as we attend this special Christmas concert. Do you remember going last year and how much each of us enjoyed hearing the Christmas songs the group sang? We hope to make this a yearly tradition. Get all dressed up for our special evening together. We're going to have such fun!

We kept our eyes out for a good buy on concert tickets for our family. There are many holiday concerts and performances that you could find tickets for if you start looking early. This is a good opportunity to teach the younger children the importance of good manners. It's always fun to dress up a little more than we normally would and go out to something special. We offered babysitters for the very young children so the parents could enjoy the evening without stress.

On the NINTH Day of

Christmas

We bring to you with love . . .

Imagine . . . coloring books with lots of elf pictures! What a fun evening for you to be together as a family and coloring pictures of darling little elves. Mom and Dad, remember that it is important for you to color with the children. They will love it! We have included new crayons and magic markers for you also. Have fun!

Coloring with our children is such fun, and there are some wonderful coloring books from which to choose. We looked for those with lots of pictures of elves so it would go along with the theme. We were careful to make sure our magic markers were washable. The moms in the family will definitely appreciate that!

On the TENTH Day of

Christmas

We bring to you with love . . .

Imagine . . . an elf stocking! Yes, you now have an elf stocking to hang on Christmas Eve for Santa to fill with lots of goodies. We know how much you love the new elf that has come to visit you during the Christmas holidays so this will be especially fun to have a stocking that will remind you of him. We're sure your elf will be pleased to see this. We are hoping each one of you gets lots of good things you are wanting this Christmas. Oh, how we love you!

✻ ✻ ✻ ✻ ✻

I found the pattern for the elf stockings on the Internet, and they were quite easy to make. Our grandchildren thought these stockings were the perfect way to show how much they love their little elf.

Instructions for Elf Stocking

Things you will need:
2 pieces of light green fleece, each 24 x 20 inches
3 pieces of dark green felt, each 24 x 20 inches
Dark green embroidery floss
Red or gold jingle bells, 4 medium plus 1 large for toe
Small amount of Fiberfill
8 to 9 inches of red twisted cording

* Cut 1 boot shape from each piece of the light green fleece.
* Cut a decorative shape from 1 piece of the dark green felt for the front of the stocking and 1 stocking shape from each of the remaining two pieces of the felt.
* Place a light green boot on top of a dark green boot. Pin the decorative shape on top and use the floss to whipstitch around the inner edge of decorative shape through both boots.
* Pin together all 4 boots with the dark green boots on the inside.
* Using the floss, whipstitch around the edges, sewing the boots together. Do not sew the top edges.

* At the top, sew together the front 2 edges, then the back 2.
* Fold down the top to make a cuff.
* Sew the medium-sized bells to the decorative shape and the large red bell to the tip of the toe.
* Tape the ends of the cord to keep them from fraying, then sew the cording to the stocking for hanging.
* Stuff the curly toe of the boot with fiberfill to keep it from flopping over when the stocking is empty.

On the ELEVENTH Day of

Christmas

We bring to you with love . . .

Imagine . . . a surprise being delivered to you today! Be looking for NeNa and PaPa to arrive this afternoon with a delicious surprise for you! You're going to love it. We can hardly wait to see you and give you our "elf" surprise. Santa will also be visiting you tonight and he will be bringing you lots of surprises. What a wonderful day!

❄ ❄ ❄ ❄ ❄

We arrived at the home of each family with a plate of elf cookies all decorated and, boy, were they ever appreciated. I found the elf cookie cutters in a kitchen specialty store and bought enough to tie a cookie cutter to each plate of cookies. I put the cookies on a pretty plate, wrapped cellophane around the plate, and tied a bow at the top. This is where I added the cookie cutter so they could make more cookies during the holidays. They enjoyed having a fresh baked treat and having the cookies in the shape of their new friend, the elf, was such fun. I frosted them with green and red icing, and they were adorable. If you will be mailing your gifts, why not send the cookie cutters, the recipe, and a can of frosting? You can also consider sending the dry packaged cookie mix. Cookies are always wonderful to receive in any form!

On the TWELFTH Day of
Christmas
We bring to you with love . . .

Imagine . . . a new DVD! You will have lots of laughs together as a family tonight as you watch your new DVD called *Elf*. It stars Will Ferrell. What a great story and it can be enjoyed by all ages. We have included some of your favorite candy to enjoy as you watch the movie. Did Santa take your special elf back to the North Pole last night when he came to your house? Elves are needed all year to help Santa make toys and they love making special ones just for you. Treasure the wonderful memories you have of your elf and look forward to his return next Christmas. Merry Christmas to each one of you! You bring us so much happiness at this special time of the year. How blessed we are to be sharing this beautiful holiday with you.

❄ ❄ ❄ ❄ ❄

This DVD is a great story and is sure to be a favorite among your family. There is another DVD you might consider called The Happy Elf. *DVDs are great for mailing and make wonderful gifts. Hey, maybe you'll even be invited over to watch it with them.*

Each year, our children prepare some kind of response to the 12 Days of Christmas and this year was such a fun one. They presented Sterling and me with a darling book they had put together showing pictures of their elves doing some of the fun things they did while visiting their homes during Christmas. What a treasure for us! There were comments from the grandchildren telling of their delight in each of their gifts and telling how much they love their little elf. We had experienced another amazing 12 Days of Christmas.

Chapter Five

It's "Snow" Much Fun to Be with You!

The aging process has you firmly in its grasp if you never get the urge to throw a snowball.

Doug Larson

This truly was a Christmas to remember! We had wonderful times together as a family and made memories that will last forever. There is nothing quite like playing in the snow with little ones or watching them as they fly down the hill on their sleds and listening to their laughter when they reach the bottom or end up in a snowbank. We always tried to have a camera handy to capture these memories. Our children and grandchildren consider this to have been one of their favorite years. Do you think this theme will work for you family? You'll have "snow" much fun planning the 12 Days of Christmas and sharing the excitement with your children and grandchildren! Beware . . . you may have to dodge some snowballs!

On the FIRST Day of
Christmas
We bring to you with love . . .

A New Sled! We know how much you love sledding, so today you are getting a new sled to try out on your favorite hill. This sled seemed to be the perfect color and size for your family to enjoy together. Won't this be lots of fun! Be sure to dress warmly so you can stay outside for a long time. Have fun! We will be thinking of you.

❄ ❄ ❄ ❄ ❄

We tried to find a sled that was a little different. The discount stores have lots to choose from so you'll easily find one you like. Mailing your gift? Why not send a gift card telling them to have a family outing and pick out the sled they like best. The children would love that. You can always adjust these ideas to make them work for your family.

On the SECOND Day of
Christmas
We bring to you with love . . .

A new scarf! NeNa has been busy making these wonderful fleece scarves for each one of you. Now you can stay nice and warm when you go outside to ride your new sleds. We want to come sledding with you so we can take some pictures of you wearing your new scarves. Playing in the snow together will be lots of fun. Oh, how we love you!

❄ ❄ ❄ ❄ ❄

I actually made the simplest scarves I could so it would be a quick but useful project. I bought some wonderful patterns of fleece for the younger children and stripes and plaids for the ones a little older, especially the parents. I'll include how I made mine, but you may want to look for a more detailed pattern.

Layer 2 pieces of fleece (I like the micro fleece best) using coordinating colors if you like the look. Cut fleece into strips of approximately 8 inches wide depending on the size you want. You will determine the length by the size of the person for whom you are making the scarf. Remember that the stretch in the fabric should run the length of your scarf. Sew a straight stitch down the center of the scarf lengthwise and reinforce it so it will hold. Next, cut ½ inch strips in from the long edge into about 1 inch from the seam you have previously sewn. Do that for the length of the scarf on both sides, being careful to keep the fleece straight. Tie a knot at the end of each piece of fringe for a fun look. By using 2 pieces of fleece you will be assured that the scarf will be warm for those cold, snowy days when the children are playing outside.

On the THIRD Day of
Christmas
We bring to you with love . . .

A Snowball Maker! You're going to love this new toy! It will make lots of snowballs for any snowball fight. Plus, it will help keep your gloves a little dryer. Your snowball maker will make soft, safe snowballs. Sometimes the snowballs made by hand can be very hard and can really hurt when you get hit! Have fun playing outside in the snow! Remember, snowball fights should be fun, so be careful that you don't hurt anyone.

✳ ✳ ✳ ✳ ✳

We found the snowball makers at our local franchise store and later saw them at several other stores in town and on the Internet. They shouldn't be hard to find and aren't hard to mail to families. Our grandchildren loved them and had such fun. The ones we found were about six or seven dollars, so watch for the sales.

On the FOURTH Day of
Christmas
We bring to you with love . . .

Hot Chocolate Mix and Scones! We know you're going to need some hot chocolate to warm those little tummies after an afternoon of playing in the snow, so we're giving you your favorite flavor. NeNa and PaPa will be showing up with some fresh scones. Isn't that going to make a yummy treat for you! We're thinking of you!

✳ ✳ ✳ ✳ ✳

Because of the many choices of hot chocolate mix, you'll surely find one you'll want to give. If you don't live close enough to your family to deliver fresh scones, perhaps mailing your gifts could be the answer. Include a recipe for scones and some toppings. You could also send a cookie mix that they could make together after a fun day of playing in the snow.

Scones

2 cups boiling water

½ cup sugar

1 cube butter

1 tsp. salt

2 pkgs. dry yeast

flour

Dissolve sugar, butter, and salt in the hot water. Cool slightly; add the yeast. Mix these ingredients together. Add enough flour to make a sticky dough. Knead for 5–10 minutes. Cover and let rise once. Punch down and shape into a ball. Cover and let rise again. Roll out on lightly floured board (¼-in. thick). Cut into strips. Cover and let rise again. Deep-fry and lay out on paper towels for a minute or two. Serve with honey butter, jam, syrup, or any of your favorite toppings.

On the FIFTH Day of

Christmas

We bring to you with love . . .

A Snow Fort/Igloo Maker! This is going to be "snow" much fun! You can make a wonderful snow fort with this block maker. The snow is packed into the plastic form and then when you push the release switch, it will dump out the block of snow. It will be ready to place anywhere you want. You can stack the blocks as high as you want. Be sure and invite us over to see what you have made. Maybe Mom and Dad will want to be included in this project. You'll also want to ask them to take some pictures of the fort. We can imagine you in your new fort having lots of fun. Your cousins will want to visit your fort to see how successful you are.

❄ ❄ ❄ ❄ ❄

The snow fort/igloo makers are found in franchise stores, or you can also find them on the Internet and have them shipped to you. We found this to be one of the most fun projects ever for the grandchildren. They were very proud of what they had made and were anxious to show off the finished project. The snow fort/igloo makers usually sell for about five to seven dollars, but you can always watch for sales.

On the SIXTH Day of
Christmas
We bring to you with love . . .

A Snow Globe! Isn't this a beautiful snow globe, especially since it has your picture in it! We chose a picture of you playing in the snow so it will be a reminder each year of the fun you have as you play with your friends and family in the snow. You can change the picture each year as you get older. This will be a great keepsake for you and your family.

I felt very fortunate to have found these snow globes in a print shop. I knew right away that this would work perfectly with our theme. It could be turned upside down and the snow would fall all around the picture. We sorted through our pictures and found one of each family that suited the snow globe just right. There are many beautiful snow globes to choose from, so maybe you'll find one with a snowman, children sledding, or one that will suit your needs better. After Christmas is a perfect time to shop for gifts like this and then hide them away until next year. Just don't be like me and forget where you put them!

On the SEVENTH Day of
Christmas
We bring to you with love . . .

A Snowman Ornament! Today you are receiving a new ornament for your memory tree. This adorable snowman ornament won us over the first time we saw it. We knew right away that we had to make one for you. Your ornament is called "Once There Was a Snowman." As you look at it each year, it will be the perfect memory of our theme for this year. Yes, it is, indeed, "snow" much fun being with you. Tonight as you hang your new ornament on your memory tree, we hope you will take time as a family to recall the time spent making wonderful memories together in the snow. We are very blessed to have families that love us. We love each one of you with all our hearts!

✳ ✳ ✳ ✳ ✳

These ornaments truly are darling! Our daughter showed these to me and I loved them right away. Let me give you the instructions so you can put one together and see what you think. I hope you'll find them to be as darling as I do.

"Once There Was a Snowman" Ornament

* Purchase clear round glass ornaments, tiny black beads, and Wonder Water.
* Paint the tip end of a toothpick orange—about ¼ inch from the end. Break the ¼ inch off and set it aside.
* Remove hanger end from the ornament.
* Pour approximately ½ inch of Wonder Water into ornament. Mix Wonder Water per instructions on bottle. Use a small funnel to pour Wonder Water into ornament.
* Sprinkle small amount of glitter on top of Wonder Water to give a glisten to the snow.
* Drop the end of the toothpick (snowman's nose) and 2 black beads (snowman's eyes) into the ornament. You may need to use a small stick to place the black beads close together. Replace the top to the ornament. Tie a small ribbon through the top for a hanger. You now have a melted snowman!
* Store upright until the Wonder Water has firmly set. Keep the container the ornaments came in so you can store them in the container during the year. The Wonder Water will have a tendency to slide if left tilted to one side for very long.

Runaway Snowball

Someone in the sky last night
had an awful pillow fight,
And when I woke today I found

all the snowflakes on the ground.
I made myself a snowball
as perfect as could be,
I thought I'd keep it
as a pet and let it sleep with me.
I made it some pajamas
and a pillow for its head,
Then last night it ran away
but first . . .
it wet my bed!
Little snowflakes so soft and white,
falling silently during the night,
glistening in the sun today
makes us want to come out and play.
We'll build a snowman or maybe two,
which wouldn't be possible, without you.
Pretty soon though, you will melt
but we'll always remember just how we felt,
The day the snow came tumbling down
and covered every street in town.

Author Unknown

On the EIGHTH Day of
Christmas
We bring to you with love . . .

Snowman Lollipops! Once again, you are receiving lollipops for you and your best friends. We love your comments each year as you share a lollipop with your friends. We never want to be unkind to our friends in any way. Always appreciate them and show your appreciation by the way you treat them. Since many of you requested a few extra lollipops for your many friends, we are giving you lots of extras. It's wonderful to make new friends and to have plenty of friends but never, ever forget the friends you have made in the past. Remember, we build on friendships. These friendships will prove to be real treasures in your lives as you grow older. We made lots of delicious flavors so enjoy them! You are "snow" much fun to be with! No wonder you have so many friends!

❄ ❄ ❄ ❄ ❄

The lollipops have become a tradition each year, and we love the fact that our grandchildren look forward to sharing lollipops with their friends and telling them that they are a great friend. We are trying to reinforce the value of friendship each year with the giving of the lollipops. You can find all shapes, flavors, and sizes of lollipops in many stores or, if you choose, you can make your own. The flavoring, sticks, molds, bags, and decorations can be found in most craft stores.

Lollipop Recipe

2 cups sugar
1 cup light corn syrup
½ cup water
1 tsp. flavoring
Food coloring to make desired color

Combine sugar, corn syrup, and water. Stir until sugar dissolves. Let boil without stirring until mixture reaches 300 degrees. Meanwhile, prepare molds by spraying with non-stick spray and laying them on a lightly greased marble slab or cookie sheet. Insert sticks into molds. When mixture has reached 300 degrees, remove from heat. Let cool to 280 degrees. Stir in flavoring and desired amount of food coloring. Pour mixture into molds and let set until completely cool. Remove lollipop from mold and place in a lollipop baggie. Secure with tape.

Day #9

On the NINTH Day of

Christmas

We bring to you with love . . .

A Snowman Kit! Hopefully you are getting lots of snow this year so that you will be able to make good use of this gift. Your snowman kit includes everything you will need to build a fabulous snowman. All you have to add is the snow! There is a black hat, scarf, pipe, wooden carrot, and some coal for his eyes. We've also included big buttons for the front of your snowman. You are going to have the best-looking snowman in town. Have fun in the snow and remember . . . it's "snow" much fun to be with you. We will be stopping by to see your snowman. We love you!

❄ ❄ ❄ ❄ ❄

This idea was definitely a huge hit with everyone. While shopping in a boutique in the fall, we found these darling snowman kits. We knew right away that our families would love this. You can also find these kits on the Internet. Order them early and have them ready to give to your special families. It's another easy gift for mailing! Use this opportunity to make special memories with your children and grandchildren by playing in the snow with them. They will tell the stories many times throughout the years of the fun they had playing in the snow with someone so special to them.

On the TENTH Day of

Christmas
We bring to you with love . . .

A Snow Cone Maker! Many times during the year we have shared snow cones together, so we know how much you love them. Now you have your very own snow cone maker and can make them any time you want. We have included several flavors of syrup for you to choose from, so get together as a family and share some snow cones today. It's "snow" much fun to surprise you! Have fun and remember how much you are loved!

❄ ❄ ❄ ❄ ❄

We did some shopping around to find a snow cone maker that would be durable and also easy for the children to use. One of the best buys was in a franchise store and they were actually on sale. You should be able to find a good snow cone maker for about $20 to $40. There are more expensive ones that may suit your needs more. Check on the Internet also. It's a good way to buy the snow cone maker and have it delivered to your family if they live away. The cones and syrups are sold separately, so your family can get more supplies as they need them.

On the ELEVENTH Day of

Christmas

We bring to you with love . . .

Snowball Cookies! You're "snow" going to love your treat today! We found a yummy new recipe and it's a perfect treat for our "snow" theme. Try some of these snowball surprise cookies and see if you agree with us that these are delicious. Hey, could there be anything more perfect than snowball cookies for our snow theme? Eat lots of them and remember to share.

❉ ❉ ❉ ❉ ❉

This is a wonderful recipe that I knew my family would like. Children like nothing better than a plate of fresh cookies with instructions to eat as many as they want. If you are mailing your gifts, consider sending a small book of your favorite recipes. Any family would like that. You could make your recipe book as simply or as fancy as you like. You could write them on recipe cards and put them into a small photo book. This would be a quick and inexpensive way to share your recipes and, yet, would be a great keepsake for anyone.

Snowball Surprises

8 oz. unsalted butter, softened

¾ cup sugar

1 tsp. vanilla extract

2 cups sifted all-purpose flour

30 chocolate kisses, unwrapped

Powdered sugar

Cream the butter and sugar until fluffy. Add vanilla. Add flour and continue to mix well. Wrap in plastic wrap and refrigerate for about 30 minutes. Remove dough from refrigerator and break into balls large enough to cover a chocolate kiss. Insert the kiss and wrap dough around it, making sure the kiss is completely covered. Bake on ungreased cookie sheet in 350 degree preheated oven for approximately 10 to 12 minutes. Remove cookies from baking sheet to cooling rack. While still warm, sift powdered sugar over the cookies. Cool completely. Makes 2½ dozen.

On the TWELFTH Day of

Christmas

We bring to you with love . . .

New Slippers! Oh, we can't help thinking of your cold toes after you have played in the snow for a while. We chose to give you fluffy slippers that are promised to warm up your feet quickly. You know NeNa and PaPa don't want you to be cold, so put on your new slippers and sit by the fire until you are warm. Maybe you could enjoy a cup of hot chocolate while you're warming up. We will be thinking of you.

☀ ☀ ☀ ☀ ☀

Slippers are very easy to find, and you can usually find them in just about any size and color you want. We found some wonderful ones in animal shapes and the grandchildren loved them. Be looking for sales and you'll surely find them. This is another gift that is easily mailed.

When it snows you have two choices: shovel or make snow angels.

Unknown author

Chapter Six

No Empty Chairs

A happy home is but an earlier heaven. Do we want our homes to be happy? If we do, let them be the abiding place of prayer, thanksgiving, and gratitude.

GEORGE ALBERT SMITH

A dear friend came to me one day with great excitement to tell me about a CD she had heard. She felt sure I would love it. As I listened to the song, I became filled with the most beautiful feelings, and I knew right away that this was to be our theme for the 12 Days of Christmas. Nothing touches my heart quite like music, especially music about families, and this was no exception. I listened to the words over and over and was more touched each time I heard them. My family means more to me than words could ever express, and I'm sure you feel the same way about your family. I can't begin to imagine my family with a single person missing from the circle. Years of prayers and pleadings in behalf of each child have been spent with the faith and belief that we, as a family, can always be together. I never want there to be even *one* empty chair at our eternal table. Challenges come into our lives, as we know they will, but we hold tight to that goal. A parent knows the emptiness that comes with the first day the family gathers around the table after a son or daughter has left for college or when a missionary is faithfully serving in another state or country. Along with the joy of seeing children marry, we face a temporary empty chair. They return home, on occasion, bringing with them new family members to join us at our table. A peaceful feeling fills my heart when I acknowledge that we are an eternal family and, hopefully, one day will be joined around an eternal table. Then I have the solace I need, but I know I must continue working toward my eternal goal—to have no empty chairs at our eternal table. As you know, this is an everyday effort.

On the FIRST Day of

Christmas

We bring to you with love . . .

Bring Music to the Table! A new CD! Senator Orrin Hatch and Janice Kapp Perry have produced a CD that is absolutely amazing. One of our favorite songs on the CD is "No Empty Chairs." We are reminded of the importance of having all our family together and that we need to stay close as a family. There will be times when members of our family will be away and their chair will be empty, but we look forward to their return and know we can be a forever family. Listen to your CD together and pay close attention to the beautiful words. We are thankful to have such a wonderful family as you!

❄ ❄ ❄ ❄ ❄

You may have to order the CD, so allow time for that. Several songs on the CD will touch your heart and could lead to themes for the 12 Days of Christmas in future years. Also, mailing the CD will be easy.

No Empty Chairs

Look around our family table, every person in his place
Memorize this happy moment, and each familiar face.
Look around our family table, feel the love that we all share,
Life is sweet and so complete, with each loved one gathered here.
There are no empty chairs at our table, no empty feelings inside
When all those we love are together, here side by side.
Time will fly, and all too quickly, some will leave to try their wings
Empty places at our table, will tug at our heart strings.
But the number at our table, will increase as children come
Bringing to our family table, sweet innocence and fun.
We'll add a few more chairs to our table, a lot more laughter and love

As our joy is multiplied daily, to fill our cups.
When there comes a time for parting, there will be no tears because
We will set a grander table, where all may live in love.
There we'll wait for each dear loved one, who will come to take his
    place,
At the feast that lasts forever, in God's eternal place.
We'll have no empty chairs at our table, no empty feeling inside,
When all those we love are together, there side by side.
May the circle not be broken, may each one return to be,
Safe within this peaceful haven, through all eternity.
We'll have no empty chairs at our table, when all are gathered above,
No more empty chairs at our table, in heaven's home of love.

On the SECOND Day of

Christmas

We bring to you with love . . .

Bring Compassion to the Table! A new apron for Mom! NeNa made this cute apron for you to wear during the holidays. Maybe you have some memories of visiting your grandmother and seeing her wear an apron. Do you remember the many ways she would use it? We don't often use aprons today in all the many ways they were used years ago. We do wear them still to protect our clothing while baking. Many compassionate acts involve putting on our aprons and getting to work! Maybe you could bake something delicious while wearing your new apron and share it with a neighbor. Being compassionate is a wonderful trait. We have included some new oven mitts to go with your apron. Also, we hope you will read the apron story together. It brought tender memories . . . and some tears . . . to my mind of my wonderful grandmothers.

✳ ✳ ✳ ✳ ✳

There are many adorable aprons, and they're easy to find during the holidays. We looked for one that would be especially cute for Christmas. You'll also find patterns on the Internet and in your local fabric stores along with great Christmas prints. You are sure to get lots of hugs when you give this gift. It is a gift that will be especially easy for mailing.

Grandma's Apron

I don't think our kids know what an apron is. The principal use of Grandma's apron was to protect the dress underneath, since she only had a few. It was easier to wash aprons than dresses, and they used less material. But along with that, it served as a potholder for removing hot pans from the oven. It was wonderful for drying children's tears, and on occasion was even used for cleaning out dirty ears. From the chicken coop, the apron was used for carrying eggs, fussy chicks, and sometimes half-hatched eggs to finish in the warming oven.

When company came, those aprons were ideal hiding places for shy kids. And when the weather was cold, Grandma wrapped it around her arms. Those big old aprons wiped many a perspiring brow, bent over the hot wood stove. Chips and kindling wood were brought into the kitchen in that apron.

From the garden, it carried all sorts of vegetables. After the peas had been shelled, it carried out the hulls. In the fall, the apron was used to bring in apples that had fallen from the trees.

When unexpected company drove up the road, it was surprising how much furniture that old apron could dust in a matter of seconds.

When dinner was ready, Grandma walked out onto the porch, waved her apron, and the men knew it was time to come in from the fields to dinner.

It will be a long time before someone invents something that will replace that "old-time apron" that served so many purposes.

Author Unknown

On the THIRD Day of
Christmas
We bring to you with love . . .

Bring Wisdom to the Table! A beautiful plaque for your home is your gift today. We made this especially for your family. It has your family name in large letters with the charge to "Be True to Who You Are and the Family Name You Bear." President Gordon B. Hinckley gave us this challenge in one of his talks a few years ago, and it has always touched my heart. We hope you will remember the challenge you have to honor your family name. May each of us always try to live a life that will bring honor and respect to our name. Find a place in your home where you can hang your plaque so it may be seen each day by your family.

❋ ❋ ❋ ❋ ❋

We cut a piece of wood 24 inches long and 8 inches wide. We sanded the wood until we got it smooth enough to paint and then painted the wood dark brown and let it dry completely. It was then ready to be distressed on the sides and edges. This was done by hand with a piece of sand paper. We previously ordered vinyl lettering in off-white for the family name and tan for the saying to go across the name. We placed the family name on the wood first and then put the title "Be True to Who You Are and the Family Name You Bear" across the name. The letters for the family name were approximately 6 inches tall and the other saying was 3 inches tall. The plaque could either be hung on the wall or placed on an easel.

On the FOURTH Day of
Christmas
We bring to you with love . . .

Bring Nourishment to the Table! Freshly baked Dilly Casserole bread will be delivered to you today. This is a wonderful recipe and one we think you will enjoy. Hopefully, it will bring back memories of home and the smell of this delicious bread. We'll bring it while it is still warm so all you will need is some butter. Yummy!

❄ ❄ ❄ ❄ ❄

This bread is wonderful and very easy to make. It will be a special treat for your family and one they will want to make and share with others. I included the recipe for the Dilly Casserole Bread and also a recipe for Pumpkin Chocolate Chip Bread, in case the family might prefer a sweeter bread. Remember, if you are mailing your gifts, you can send the recipe along with a new round baking pan. What a lovely gift for your wonderful family!

Dilly Casserole Bread

¼ cup warm water

1 pckg. Dry Yeast

2 Tbsp. sugar

1 cup cottage cheese, creamed style and heated to lukewarm

1 Tbsp. minced onion

1 Tbsp. butter

2 tsp. dill seed

1 tsp. salt

¼ tsp. baking soda

1 unbeaten egg

2¼–2½ cups all-purpose flour

Dissolve sugar and yeast in water. Combine in mixing bowl: cottage cheese, onion, butter, dill seed, salt, soda, egg. Add yeast mixture. Add flour to form stiff dough. Place in round, lightly-greased baking pan, cover, and let rise until doubled in size (approx. 1 hour). Bake at 350 degrees for 40 to 50 minutes or until golden brown. Remove from oven and brush with soft butter and sprinkle lightly with salt. Makes one round loaf.

Pumpkin Chocolate Chip Bread

3½ cups flour

3 cups sugar

1 tsp. salt

1 tsp. soda

1 tsp. cinnamon

1 tsp. nutmeg

½ cup oil

½ cup water

2 cups pumpkin

4 eggs

12 oz. chocolate chips

Mix all ingredients together. Spray loaf pans. Bake at 350 degrees for 1 hour for large loaf pans and 45 minutes for small loaf pans.

On the FIFTH Day of

Christmas

We bring to you with love . . .

Bring Fun to the Table! PaPa made a dreidel for each member of your family! A dreidel is a small wooden spinning top. We have some great fun planned for you. Tonight we are inviting all of our family members for a get-together at our home. We will be having one of your favorite dinners . . . pizza! After we, eat we will have a "dreidel spin-off." Each family will have dreidels in the color of their Indian tribe. Each member of the family will have a dreidel designed especially for them. In other words, each dreidel will be decorated differently so you can always know which one is yours. You'll want to practice a lot today so you will be able to spin your dreidel and have it continue for a long time . . . making you the winner of the contest. The longest spinning dreidel wins! It's going to be lots of fun and we'll have prizes for the winners. We love you!

❄ ❄ ❄ ❄ ❄

Sterling bought toy wheels 1½ inches wide and axel pegs 1⅜ inches long. He painted the toy wheels and added some details to each one, making them all different and able to be identified by each person. He also sprinkled some of the wheels with glitter so that when they were spinning, they looked especially pretty. The wheels were allowed to dry, and then he added glue to the axel and inserted it into the wheel. When the wheel was dry, the dreidel was ready to spin and compete to be the best dreidel in our family! If you don't live close to your family, you can easily mail the dreidels and perhaps include a few prizes. The dreidel contests proved to be such fun and will definitely be used again during the year. The grandchildren assured us they will be practicing to become the dreidel champ of our family! Another beautiful memory was made with the promise of more to come. Brynlee, our six-year-old granddaughter, proved to be a true competitor. She won the grand prize!

On the SIXTH Day of

Christmas

We bring to you with love . . .

Bring Service to the Table! Today will be a wonderful day for all of us. We are going to have a day of service. PaPa and NeNa bought some small wooden cars for you to paint. There are lots of bright colored paints here for you to use. When they are dry, we will put axles and wheels on the cars and get them ready to give to some children in need. This is what makes our family stronger. Service is an important quality for us to develop. We hope you will always serve others in every way you can. You have beautiful, giving hearts. You make our hearts happy as we watch you serve. We'll have a wonderful day together as we prepare these little cars to give to those in need.

❆ ❆ ❆ ❆ ❆

Any form of service can be done. Participating together in service brings great rewards and helps teach our children the importance of serving others. You can find these small unfinished cars in most craft stores. We used craft paints in great colors for the cars. The axles and wheels were also purchased at our local craft store. This project may be a little more costly than some others, but it's rewarding to know there will be children with a new toy car for Christmas. Check with your local Humanitarian Center for free patterns of other projects you may want to consider.

On the SEVENTH Day of
Christmas
We bring to you with love . . .

Bring Unity to the Table! Oh, how we love sticky pull-apart bread! But . . . today we want to encourage you to *never* "pull apart" as a family but rather to always stick together. Be a strong member in your family circle and strengthen others. We love watching you as you strive to increase the unity within your family. Enjoy your pull-apart bread and pour yourself a big glass of milk to go along with it. Now that's got to be delicious!

❄ ❄ ❄ ❄ ❄

We delivered this bread to their homes after the grandchildren had returned from school. This has always been one of our families' favorite treats, so we knew they would love it. I have included the recipe below.

Sticky Pull-Apart Bread

¾ cup sugar

3 tsp. cinnamon

2 cans refrigerator buttermilk biscuits

1 stick butter

¾ cup dark brown sugar, packed

⅔ cup chopped nuts

Stir together sugar and cinnamon in a separate bowl. Cut biscuits into quarter pieces and roll in sugar mixture. Place into greased Bundt pan, stacking the dough in rows. Add any remaining sugar and cinnamon mixture on top. In sauce pan, combine butter and brown sugar and heat to full boil. Stir in nuts. Pour over top of biscuits. Bake at 350 degrees for 25 to 30 minutes. Let cool in pan on rack for 10 minutes.

On the EIGHTH Day of

Christmas

We bring to you with love . . .

Bring Support to the Table! Today we are giving a matching tie to each boy in your family and a matching necklace to each girl. On the first Sunday of each month, we will all wear our matching ties and necklaces. This will be our effort to show support for our family. On this day we will think of our family and pray for each individual person, especially those who may be in need. Families should think of one another and pray for one another. Each one of you is a special gift to our family.

A wonderful friend of mine, Marilyn Harmer, told me about her family doing this and shared with me the special feelings it has brought in uniting her family. I often thought about this and wondered if this might be something through which our family could grow closer. I found matching ties for all the men in a Christmas boutique and a matching necklace for each girl in a department store. They were adorable. The family thought this was a great idea, and each month we feel a special closeness to one another as we wear our ties and necklaces. As I have said before, I always have my eyes and ears open for ideas to share with our family. My friends are such great examples to me, and I'm forever indebted to them.

On the NINTH Day of

Christmas

We bring to you with love . . .

Bring Memories to the Table! What a fun evening we have planned for you! Tonight we will all join together at NeNa and PaPa's home for an evening of sharing our favorite Christmas stories. Put on your pajamas and slippers, and grab your favorite blanket so you can curl up by the fire and listen as members of our family tell memories of Christmases. We each have wonderful memories that are dear to us, so tonight we will be sharing them. There will be lots of popcorn to share also. We can hardly wait to see you and spend time together.

❈ ❈ ❈ ❈ ❈

We asked several members of our family to come prepared to share stories and memories of their most favorite Christmas. We knew we couldn't hold the attention of the little ones for too long, but, surprisingly, their little ears were tuned in to the stories. They quietly listened to stories that are a great part of their heritage. We closed the evening with the following stories.

Little Ole' Donkey That Had Little to Say

It was the night before Christmas when all the beasts came together from the farthest places of the earth to talk. The first voice to be heard was the deep, rich bass of the lion. "I speak," he said, "as king of beasts." Truly he looked a king with his beautiful thick mane and his tawny, rippling muscles. "I won't repeat my good deeds. I shall not again tonight repeat the shining stories of the days when the Romans loved me. I shall not recall the story of the one man, Daniel, who defied me in my own den—a story humbling to me—which I have often told you to prove I am not proud. I shall say nothing of my stealthy fur that makes the whole continent tremble at the very sound of my name."

"Then I shall speak," and by the trumpet sound, the beasts knew the elephant spoke. "I am the biggest beast on earth. My size and strength awe nations. Yet I can walk so softly and lightly that no ear can hear my coming. Isn't that something to be proud of? And I don't believe any of you can flip a tremendous teak log over your shoulder as handily as I can. That takes power. Yes, and who else here has been a beast of war? Who else has crossed the Alps. You know how very high the Alps are! I and my strong brothers helped the famous General Hannibal and his soldiers over them in one of his great campaigns, and Hannibal is in history books all over the world."

A strange whispering voice broke in. "You know me, the giraffe. Usually I stay silent, but I hope you will remember I am the tallest and can look down on you. But please don't think I am bragging because I am up here above you. I eat from the tops of trees. Nobody else here can do that. Besides, being the tallest, I can run faster than most."

"Let me interrupt." It was the leopard's voice. "You'd have to move very fast to outrun certain striped and spotted cousins of mine who hold most of the speed records. Right, cousins?" The tiger nodded his head and the cheetah, fastest of all, smiled.

The camel till now had been chewing his cud and watching with sad eyes. He cleared his throat and his voice rasped out, "I am neither handsome nor fleet. I have some trouble keeping clean. But I have the right to feel proud as anyone here. I helped build the pyramids of Egypt! Have any of you ever tackled a job as big? Also, I am the only animal in the world that can have two humps on his back. I am used to going many days without water, across scorching sands that would burn the feet off most of you within hours. My friends, the camel counts, and I have a right to feel happy!"

For a long while after the camel's speech, there was a silence. Then the llama coughed and said, "I am, by nature, modest. One thing, however, I have had much experience crossing mountains. You have heard of the Andes, my home, and the war work I have done."

Others spoke too. The goose honked, "I laid a golden egg once. Who else has done that?" The turtle said, "I'm the slowest. It's better. When you go fast, you go around in circles." The fox said, "I am the slyest, the trickiest and probably the brainiest of you all." The zebra said, "For confusion, I'm best. Am I white with black stripes or black with white stripes?" The grizzly bear said, "Who is heavy as I and can climb a tree as well?" The polar bear said, "Can anybody but me swim with icebergs or catch a fish with a paw?"

A little gray beast stood listening. Finally, the other animals looked his way. There wasn't much he could do but speak. "I am a donkey," he began, in a voice so hoarse and low that the other beasts leaned forward to hear. "I can't run fast or go days without water. I couldn't swim a stroke among icebergs. I've never climbed a tree. Nobody is afraid of me."

Lower and lower sank the little donkey's voice. His ears drooped and his head was bowed. The other beasts could hardly hear him. Suddenly he raised his head. His eyes looked far away in time and space and there was a strange glow around him. "Only one thing I have ever done has stuck in my mind. It happened a long, long time ago . . . on the way to Egypt in the dark of night. *I carried a mother who carried a king.*"

C. Ralph Bennett

Favorite Christmas

When I was fifteen years old, my father was called as a Building Supervisor Missionary to Germany. I was the oldest of four children, and our family packed up and moved to Darmstadt, Germany for three years.

Money was very scarce, as is the case with most missionaries, but my parents did all they could to make our stay in Germany great. Every Christmas and Easter, my dad had two weeks off from his duties. He was determined that his family would see as many of the sights as possible during that time.

One Christmas, we piled into our blue Volkswagen construction truck and headed for Austria. Our truck had two bench seats and *no heater*. My dad built each of us a small wooden stool to put our feet on instead of the cold steel floor of the truck. Each one of us, except for my dad, traveled zipped up in a mummy sleeping bag, and we passed a window scraper around as we scraped the *inside* of our truck.

We spent the night in a little attic room above a one-hundred-year-old *gasthaus* (little café). Our room had no heat and no bathroom. There was a chamber pot under one of the beds. We all piled into the two beds in the room under big feather comforters. It was freezing! We laid in those beds and sang Christmas songs most of the cold, cold night. In the morning, my dad gave each of us an unwrapped, inexpensive Edelweiss necklace.

We were able to visit the little church in Oberndorf, Austria, where the song "Silent Night" was written and first sung on Christmas Eve in 1814 to the music of a guitar because the church organ was broken.

I have experienced many beautiful Christmas seasons, but none is as cherished in my heart as was the humble Christmas we spent in Austria. We had no decorations, no tree, no heat, no bathroom, and one small gift, but it was the best Christmas ever. I don't think I was ever warm on that trip, but I feel a warm glow when I sing the beautiful song "Silent Night."

Over the years I have often wished I could give our children and our grandchildren a Christmas like that. I have come to realize that all the money in the world can't buy the real treasures in life.

Kristine Schellenberg

On the TENTH Day of
Christmas
We bring to you with love . . .

Bring Knowledge to the Table! We know how much each one of you loves to read, so today's gift is a new book. We tried to find just the right book for you. Perhaps you can trade with your cousins when you have finished your book. Parents, your book is on emergency preparedness, so you can become more knowledgeable about preparing your family for the difficult times we may face in the future. You will learn more about food storage as well as how to prepare your family for emergencies. We all need to read and be prepared. Please set some time aside after the holidays for this. The responsibility of caring and preparing for our families is one we cannot take lightly. We love you very much!

One of our favorite books on emergency preparedness is called Preparedness Principles *by Barbara Salsbury. After reading this book, you will be well informed on how to begin to prepare your family for difficult days ahead. Barbara doesn't cause panic but rather defines clearly that we can begin step by step to reach that goal we all have . . . that of caring for the ones we love. Barbara's book can be found in most bookstores.*

On the ELEVENTH Day of
Christmas
We bring to you with love . . .

Bring Goals to the Table! The white stocking you are receiving today is very special. Today, being Christmas Eve, you will hang the white stocking among your other stockings that are waiting to be filled with surprises from Santa. The white stocking is a little different. It is intended for Jesus. Tomorrow is His birthday and the stocking is to be filled with gifts *for* Him. Tonight, as you gather around your Christmas tree, express your feelings about the birth of the Savior of the world, what His birth means to you, and your love for Him. Then privately write down your gift to Jesus. Your gift could include such things as your personal goals you hope to achieve throughout the next year, ways you can be of service to others, improvements you desire to make in yourself and in your relationships with family members or friends. It might be a goal to strengthen your spiritual life. When you have written your gift to Jesus, place it in the white envelope we have included. Everyone will place their sealed envelope with their name on it in the white stocking to be reviewed next Christmas Eve. At that time, each person will read their gift from the past year, write a new gift to the Savior, and place it in the white stocking again. Hopefully, this will be a more meaningful year for you as you contemplate your gift to the Master.

❄ ❄ ❄ ❄ ❄

This gift required very little preparation but proved to be extremely meaningful. We all like to feel we are giving something back to our Savior in some way. White stockings are easy to find and make a great gift for easy mailing.

Day #12

On the TWELFTH Day of

Christmas

We bring to you with love . . .

Bring Friendship to the Table! What a fun treat we have for you today! Each one will receive two plastic candy canes filled with M&M's. This year you will have one for yourself and the other one you are to give to your best friend. Just as we have done in the past with the lollipops, this year you will express your love and gratitude to your friend for their friendship. Tell them what a great friend they are to you. We love our friends and need to tell them so. We never want to take these friendships for granted. Friendships are to be treasured and built upon. Make sure you are also a good friend! We love seeing you with your friends!

❄ ❄ ❄ ❄ ❄

In the past we have used lollipops for expressing our love and gratitude to our friends, so this year we decided to change it a little and do something different.

The grandchildren loved the M&M's and thought it was a great idea to share them with their friends. It has become important to our grandchildren to look forward to sharing this tradition with their friends.

Be slow in choosing a friend; Slower in changing.

BENJAMIN FRANKLIN

On This Day

Mend a quarrel. Search out a forgotten friend. Dismiss suspicion, and replace it with trust. Write a love letter. Share some treasure. Give a soft answer. Encourage youth. Manifest your loyalty in a word or deed. Keep a promise. Find the time. Forego a grudge. Forgive an enemy. Listen. Apologize if you were wrong. Try to understand. Flout envy. Examine your demands on others. Think first of someone else. Appreciate, be kind, be gentle. Laugh a little more. Deserve confidence. Take up arms against malice. Decry complacency. Express your gratitude. Worship your God.

Gladden the heart of a child. Take pleasure in the beauty and wonder of the earth. Speak your love. Speak it again. Speak it still again. Speak it still once again.

AUTHOR UNKNOWN

Chapter Seven

The Reason for the Season

*Live your life in such a way that those who know you but don't know
Christ, will want to know Christ because they know you.*

AUTHOR UNKNOWN

The following ideas are especially great suggestions for families who are
mailing their gifts. This theme is also good for giving to friends and neighbors
when you want to brighten their days with a loving remembrance. It takes
some preparation by shopping for the little tokens to be given each day, but we
found most everything we needed in a craft store. Dollar stores are also ideal
places to look for these items. You will first want to find a small Christmas
tree that can be set on a table or shelf. Each day a small sack is given with a
scripture typed and stapled to the top of it. After reading the scripture, open
the sack and put the ornament on the tree. This continues throughout the 12
Days of Christmas. Too often we get caught up in the hustle and bustle of the
holidays and neglect to stop and think of the reason for the season—Jesus
Christ. What a wonderful way to remember Christ each day.

On the FIRST Day of
Christmas
We bring to you with love . . .

Lights for your tree! **Psalms 27:1**—The Lord is my light and my salvation; whom shall I fear? The Lord is the strength of my life; of whom shall
I be afraid?

✳ ✳ ✳ ✳ ✳

You'll want to get the smallest set of lights you can find, since you are giving them a small tree. We found strings with only 25 light bulbs and they were perfect. These are often found in craft shops and doll house supply stores.

On the SECOND Day of
Christmas
We bring to you with love . . .

A heart to represent the love of God! **John 3:16–17**—For God so loved the world, that he gave his only begotten Son, that whosoever believeth in him should not perish, but have everlasting life. For God sent not his Son into the world to condemn the world, but that the world through him might be saved.

✳ ✳ ✳ ✳ ✳

If you check the unfinished wood section of your local craft store, you should be able to find a wooden heart that only needs to be painted. Let your imagination loose on this and you'll think of other ideas for making beautiful hearts for the tree. I especially like the jeweled hearts that glitter and sparkle.

On the THIRD Day of
Christmas
We bring to you with love . . .

Small piece of towel! **John 13:4–17**—He riseth from supper, and laid aside his garments; and took a towel, and girded himself. After that he poureth water into a bason, and began to wash the disciples feet, and to wipe them with the towel wherewith he was girded. Then cometh he to Simon Peter; and Peter saith unto him, Lord, dost thou wash my feet? Jesus answered and said unto him, What I do thou knowest not now; but thou shalt know hereafter. Peter saith unto him, Thou shalt never wash my feet.

Jesus answered him, If I wash thee not, thou hast no part with me. Simon Peter saith unto him, Lord, not my feet only, but also my hands and my head. Jesus saith to him, He that is washed needeth not save to wash his feet, but is clean every whit; and ye are clean, but not all. For he knew who should betray him; therefore said he, Ye are not all clean.

So after he had washed their feet, and had taken his garments, and was set down again he said unto them, Know ye what I have done to you? Ye call me Master and Lord; and ye say well; for so I am. If I then, your Lord and Master, have washed your feet; ye also ought to wash one another's feet. For I have given you an example, that ye should do as I have done to you. Verily, verily, I say unto you, The servant is not greater than his lord; neither he that is sent greater than he that sent him. If ye know these things, happy are ye if ye do them.

❄ ❄ ❄ ❄ ❄

Cut a small piece of terry cloth and punch a hole into one corner of the towel. Place a piece of thin white ribbon through the hole so you can use this to hang the towel on your tree.

On the FOURTH Day of

Christmas

We bring to you with love . . .

A bell! **Luke 15:4–7**—What man of you, having an hundred sheep, if he lose one of them, doth not leave the ninety and nine in the wilderness, and go after that which is lost, until he find it? And when he hath found it, he layeth it on his shoulders, rejoicing. And when he cometh home, he calleth together his friends and neighbours, saying unto them, rejoice with me; for I have found my sheep which was lost. I say unto you, that likewise joy shall be in heaven over one sinner that repenteth, more than over ninety and nine just persons, which need no repentance.

❄ ❄ ❄ ❄ ❄

We used a small bell to remind us of the sheep's bell. You could also use a small sheep to relate to this scripture. We saw some small sheep in a local craft shop. This would serve beautifully to remind us of the lost sheep and how important it is for us to go in search of them.

On the FIFTH Day of

Christmas

We bring to you with love . . .

A jar of ointment! **Luke 7: 37–38**—And, behold, a woman in the city, which was a sinner, when she knew that Jesus sat at meat in the Pharisee's house, brought an alabaster box of ointment. And stood at his feet behind him weeping, and began to wash his feet with tears, and did wipe them with the hairs of her head, and kissed his feet, and anointed them with the ointment.

❄ ❄ ❄ ❄ ❄

We used a small jar of lip balm, covered the top of the jar with a piece of muslin, and wrote "ointment" on the muslin. We used super glue to attach a piece of ribbon so it would hold the jar when it was hanging from the tree.

On the SIXTH Day of

Christmas

We bring to you with love . . .

An angel ornament! **Luke 2:9**—And, lo, the angel of the Lord came upon them, and the glory of the Lord shone round about them; and they were sore afraid. And the angel said unto them, Fear not; for, behold, I bring you good tidings of great joy, which shall be to all people. For unto you is born this day in the city of David, a Saviour, which is Christ the Lord.

❄ ❄ ❄ ❄ ❄

Angel ornaments are easy to find. You might even consider making a small crocheted angel or handkerchief angel. Homemade ornaments are always special and make wonderful keepsakes.

On the SEVENTH Day of

Christmas

We bring to you with love . . .

A nail tied with red ribbon! **Luke 23:33–34**—And when they were come to the place, which is called Calvary, there they crucified him, and the malefactors, one on the right hand, and the other on the left. Then said Jesus, Father, forgive them; for they know not what they do. And they parted his raiment, and cast lots.

❋ ❋ ❋ ❋ ❋

Using a large nail, tie a small red ribbon around the head of the nail. The ribbon will symbolize the blood that Christ shed for us. Although not the most beautiful ornament that will hang from your tree, this will be one of the most meaningful. What a perfect time of the year to remember the reason Christ came to earth and the gift He gave us.

On the EIGHTH Day of

Christmas

We bring to you with love . . .

The Wise Men's gift to the Baby Jesus. **Matthew 2:11**—And when they were come into the house, they saw the young child with Mary his mother, and fell down, and worshipped him; and when they had opened their treasures, they presented unto him gifts; gold, and frankincense, and myrrh.

❋ ❋ ❋ ❋ ❋

We found a very small gift box which we wrapped in gold paper, glued some bright colored beads on top, and added a piece of gold ribbon to the back of the box to use as a hanger. If you start looking around early enough, you may find a small chest with jewels on top, which would look great for this day's gift.

On the NINTH Day of

Christmas

We bring to you with love . . .

"JOY" ornament. **Luke 2:10–14**—When they saw the star, they rejoiced with exceeding great joy and when they were come into the house, they saw the young child, with Mary, his mother, and fell down, and worshipped him; and when they had opened their treasures, they presented unto him gifts; gold, and frankincense, and myrrh. And being warned of God in a dream that they should not return to Herod, they departed into their own country another way. And when they were departed, behold, the angel of the Lord appeareth to Joseph in a dream, saying, Arise, and take the young child, and his mother, and flee into Egypt, and be thou there until I bring thee word; for Herod will seek the young child to destroy him. When he arose, he took the young child and his mother by night, and departed into Egypt.

✳ ✳ ✳ ✳ ✳

Many craft and discount stores have this ornament among their Christmas decorations. It was quite easy for us to find.

On the TENTH Day of

Christmas

We bring to you with love . . .

A Star! **Luke 2:9–10**—When they had heard the king they departed; and, lo, the star which they saw in the East, went before them, till it came and stood over where the young child was. When they saw the star, they rejoiced with exceeding great joy.

✳ ✳ ✳ ✳ ✳

This will be one ornament you won't have any trouble finding. Stars are also easily made from wood, fabric, paper, or beads and are fun to make together as a family.

On the ELEVENTH Day of

Christmas

We bring to you with love . . .

A Picture of Christ! **Luke 2:11**—For unto you is born this day in the city of David a Saviour, which is Christ the Lord.

❄ ❄ ❄ ❄ ❄

We found a beautiful picture of Christ in a bookstore. We put it in a small frame and glued ribbon to the back of the frame so it could hang from the tree. It looked wonderful hanging on the tree with all the other ornaments.

On the TWELFTH Day of

Christmas

We bring to you with love . . .

A Fish! **Matthew 4:18–19**—And Jesus, walking by the sea of Galilee, saw two brethren, Simon called Peter, and Andrew his brother, casting a net into the sea; for they were fishers. And he saith unto them, Follow me, and I will make you fishers of men.

❄ ❄ ❄ ❄ ❄

My husband loves fishing, so I often have my eyes out for cute decorations for his office. In the past, I had seen some small fish and some of them even had a piece of jute tied around them so they could be used for tree decorations. Another idea would be to use a small piece of netting or a thin piece of wood on which you have written "Follow Me." All of these ideas fit nicely with this scripture.

Chapter Eight

Make Room for Christmas Past

What is Christmas? It is tenderness for the past, courage for the present, hope for the future. It is a fervent wish that every cup may overflow with blessings rich and eternal, and that every path may lead to peace.

AGNES M. PHARO

What better time than Christmas to think about the past and to appreciate the traditions that were made within our own families and by our ancestors? Many stories have been told and memories have been shared by those who have gone before us. They left behind their traditions of Christmas, and today, we try to capture a little of that in our holiday.

I remember my mother sharing with me the happiness her family enjoyed during Christmas. I returned with her to those wonderful days shared with her family, if only in my mind. Her memories seemed to be as fresh as they were so many years ago. She told of each Christmas Eve when she was a very young child. She would stand on the hearth of the fireplace and recite the poem, "Hang Up the Baby's Stocking." It was a precious memory throughout her life. Mother could tell a story so that you felt you were right there with her. I even imagined I could smell the food coming from the oven: the large bread pans full of cobbler made from fruit that had been bottled during the summer months; cookies and candy of every kind being made; ham baking with the smell of brown sugar and cloves. The laughter of her large family filled the air as they joined together to sing carols and prepare for Santa to make his visit. There was always the reading from the Bible of the birth of the Savior and the reminder that He was truly the reason for such a celebration as this. Then Mother climbed into a big, soft feather bed and pulled several quilts over her head. She did this to make sure Santa didn't see that she was still awake! Naturally, the quilts had been made during the cold winter months when the family stayed inside and spent time together. Oh, what a wonderful Christmas this must have been!

We love to get a glimpse of the past every chance we get. Christmas is a perfect time to share some of these traditions with our family. They need to learn of the lives of those who went before them . . . their ancestors.

We hope to touch their hearts with special memories. Our 12 Days of Christmas will be filled with stories, poems, crafts, foods, recipes, and traditions from the past. Let's pretend we are pioneers as we receive each day's gift. Wouldn't it be a fun Christmas if we could bring this to our family? We're excited to share these fun days as we "Make Room for Christmas Past."

Hang Up the Baby's Stocking

Hang up the baby's stocking
be sure you don't forget!
The dear little dimpled darling
hasn't seen Christmas yet!
But I've told her all about it
and she opened her big blue eyes,
I'm sure she understood it—
she looked so funny and wise.
Dear, what a tiny stocking!
It doesn't take much to hold,
Such little pink toe's as baby's
away from the frost and the cold.
But then, for the baby's Christmas
it will never do at all,
Why, Santa wouldn't be looking
for anything half so small.
I know what I will do for the baby
I've thought of the very best plan,
I'll borrow a stocking of Grandma's
the longest that ever I can.
And you'll hang it by mine, dear mother,
right here in the corner so!

And leave a letter to Santa
and fasten it in the toe.
Write—this is the baby's stocking
that hangs in the corner here,
You never have seen her, Santa,
for she only came this year.
But she's just the blessed'st baby
And now before you go,
Just cram her stocking with goodies
From the top clean down to the toe!

Emily Huntington Miller

On the FIRST Day of

Christmas

We bring to you with love . . .

Homemade Pomander! Families would often make pomanders to sweeten the smell within their homes. These made wonderful gifts, so families would make several to have on hand if a neighbor should drop by for a visit. We enjoy these still today. We are giving you a bag of oranges and some whole cloves along with the instructions on how to make the pomander. This is a fun project for you to make together as a family . . . just the way your ancestors did! Help Mom and Dad find the perfect place to put them, so when people come to visit during Christmas they can smell the oranges and cloves. Fragrances are a wonderful part of making our homes more beautiful, especially at Christmastime.

❄ ❄ ❄ ❄ ❄

We gave a bag of oranges, whole cloves, and some pretty ribbon from which to hang the pomanders. If you are mailing your gifts, you may want to make a couple of the pomanders to mail. Or engage the help of Mom or Dad and have them pick up oranges and cloves for you. Send a gift certificate or check to cover the cost.

Instructions for Making Pomanders

* Poke holes in orange with a fork. Cover entire orange. If you want your Pomander to last indefinitely, the **entire** piece of fruit must be covered with holes.
* Poke whole cloves into the holes you have just made. The piercings must not touch each other. There must be a space between each hole or the cloves won't stay in place.
* Roll orange and cloves in a mixture of ground cinnamon, nutmeg, and allspice.

Cure your pomander by placing the orange in an oven on very low heat for one hour. Hang the studded fruit by crisscrossing ribbon around it. Fill a basket with the oranges to make a beautiful centerpiece. The fragrance is incredible. I can picture our ancestors making wonderful memories as they made pomanders together. It seemed to be the simple things that they enjoyed most.

On the SECOND Day of

Christmas
We bring to you with love . . .

Honey Taffy! Many members of our family have never experienced the fun of pulling taffy. As you read stories about your ancestors, you hear about the times they would get together and have a taffy pull. This was great fun for them, and it brought families and friends together. We have made some honey taffy for you to eat while you make some for yourselves and for gift giving. We are excited for you to share with us the fun you had making honey taffy. Be sure to use those big muscles!

We wanted our children and grandchildren to experience the fun of pulling taffy, so we gave them the recipe and a big bottle of honey. Even the little ones participated and had great fun. This is an easy idea to mail since you can send the recipe and a bottle of honey. Just be sure to wrap the jar of honey in bubble wrap.

Honey Taffy

2 cups honey

1 cup sugar

1 cup cream

In a heavy saucepan combine all ingredients. Cook over low heat, stirring until sugar is dissolved. Continue cooking, stirring as little as possible. When mixture reaches hard ball stage (260° F) remove from heat and pour onto a shallow, buttered 9x13 inch pan. Turn edges in with a spatula to prevent candy from hardening. When just cool enough to handle, fold to center and make a long roll. Start stretching or pulling while hot. Pull until taffy becomes light and porous and small strings develop. Be sure to use buttered hands. Twist into ropes of desired thickness. With kitchen shears, cut into pieces of desired size. Wrap each piece of candy in waxed paper. This will makes about two pounds. Store in sealed container for at least two days to soften.

Honey Popcorn

1 cup heavy cream

½ cup honey

1 cup sugar

Cook to soft ball stage, pour over three bags popped microwave popcorn. Delicious!

On the THIRD Day of

Christmas

We bring to you with love . . .

Pioneer Story! Get into your comfy pajamas, grab your favorite blanket, and gather round your Christmas tree while Mom or Dad reads you the story we have enclosed. The story tells of Christmas many years ago. We are very blessed to have these stories to give us better direction for our own lives. We need to express our thankfulness in our prayers for living in a world where we have been so greatly blessed. Read the beautiful message reminding us that Christmas is Christ's birthday and not a time to ask for all the gifts we can desire. Let's pretend we are pioneers tonight as we listen closely to the story. While you listen we want you to try a bowl of Christmas Gruel. You may never have heard of this, but it was a very popular treat years ago. It's delicious—be sure and give it a try! It's good to try foods that our ancestors liked so much. I think it brings us closer to them, don't you?

✸ ✳ ✸ ✳ ✸

This was such a fun day for our family. They made the Christmas Gruel before starting the story so everyone had a bowl to enjoy while the story was being read. I typed the story on pretty Christmas paper, hoping it would be one they wanted to keep through the years. We rolled the story in scroll fashion and tied it with a pretty ribbon. It made a nice and meaningful gift!

Christmas Story

On Christmas Eve, we hung our stockings in front of the fireplace in the dining room. Father always hung a huge stocking because he assured us that Santa Claus would never get all the things he wanted in just a regular stocking. That added to the gaiety of the occasion. Each year he brought his tall rubber boots from the basement, and stood one at each side of the fireplace. No matter how excited we children were, we were never permitted to go downstairs until we were washed, combed, and fully dressed. Then we had morning prayers and sat down to breakfast—the worst breakfast of the year because it took so much time and seemed to hinder our getting to our stockings.

There was always something very unusual and very special down in the toe of the stocking. First, we laughed and laughed over the things that Santa Claus put in Father's boots—coal, kindling, and vegetables. Then we were offended because we thought Santa Claus was not very kind to Father who was always so generous with everyone else. We always brought something very special to him the next day to make up for the slight Santa Claus had made.

After our mirth and merriment had subsided, Father took us with him to make the rounds to the forgotten friends that he habitually visited on Christmas. Once we went down a long alley in the middle of a city block where there were some very poor houses. We opened the door of one tiny house and there on the bed lay an old lady, very sad and alone. As we came in, tears ran down her cheeks. She reached over to take hold of Father's hands and said, "I am grateful to you for coming because if you hadn't come,

I would have had no Christmas at all. No one else has remembered me." We thoroughly enjoyed this part of the day.

Emily Smith Stewart, daughter of George Albert Smith

December 25, 1940 It was a real treat to see how happy the children were with their gifts . . . I played with them, helped them enjoy their toys, read to them some faith-promoting stories, and we shed tears together as we had brought to our attention the sacrifices that were made by some of our loved ones when they settled this country.

Taken from the diary of George Albert Smith

My grandfather, George Albert Smith, had heard my brother, sister, and me talk about what we wanted for Christmas for weeks. We described, in detail, what we would get, what color, what size, and on and on.

Christmas Eve finally arrived and we all hung up our stockings on the fireplace mantel, still hoping aloud for *lots* of gifts.

Just before we went to bed, Grandfather said, "Wait a minute, I have to get my stocking." Pretty soon he came back with his blue eyes twinkling. He carried a great big scout sock in his hand. What's more, he had taken a pair of scissors and cut off the toe of the stocking. He hung up his stocking with great glee and then went over and got the empty coal bucket and put it right beneath the stocking.

Well, I was very impressed with how smart Grandfather was. Not only would Santa have to fill his stocking, but he'd have to fill the coal bucket too. What a smart idea!

Christmas morning, after breakfast, we opened the doors to the living room and raced in to where the tree was. I was especially anxious to see what Santa had left Grandfather.

But when I saw his stocking, my heart sank, and my eyes filled with tears, because Santa had left my very special Grandfather a switch and coal and onions.

Grandfather saw the tears in my eyes, and he pulled me towards him and said, "Now Shauna, you must remember that this is Christ's birthday we are celebrating and even Santa doesn't like to see anyone be greedy."

I learned a great lesson, one I've never forgotten and one I've always been grateful for.

Shauna Stewart Larsen,
granddaughter of George Albert Smith

Christmas Gruel

1½ cups corn meal

1½ to 2 cups sugar

1 tsp. cinnamon

nutmeg

1 pint whipping cream

Boil 6 cups water. Whisk in 1½ cups corn meal into the boiling water. Continue whisking until it thickens. Add 2 more cups water, the sugar and cinnamon, and a shake of nutmeg. Remove from heat and add whipping cream. You may need to add a little milk if mixture is too thick. Dish up and enjoy!

On the FOURTH Day of

Christmas

We bring to you with love . . .

A Punched-Out-Can Lantern! We have a great idea for you today, and it's one you can make with the help of Mom or Dad. Pioneer children used to make these to carry around or set in their room for light. These are lots of fun to make, and you'll be very proud of your finished lantern. We will be anxious to see what you have created. Pioneer children punched a tin can to decorate them and make them look pretty.

❄ ❄ ❄ ❄ ❄

This was a huge hit with all the grandchildren. They felt like real pioneers as they worked on their lanterns and were extremely proud to show them off when they were completed. Children like working together with their parents on a project, so this was a great way for them to do just that. If you are mailing your gifts, consider sending a "kit" from which they can make their lanterns. You could put all the things they would need in a box and wrap it for them to open together. Most children of all ages could participate in some way, even if they only hold the hammer and make a few hits onto the nail. I'm including the instructions for you.

Instructions for Punched-Out-Can Lanterns

Materials you will need: A 16 or 29 oz. size empty tin can, water, nail, hammer, pen or pencil, paper, masking tape, towel, black spray paint, small candle, wire for handle (optional).

* Wash your tin can and fill it with water. Place the tin can in the freezer until water has frozen solid.
* Draw your chosen design on paper large enough to go around the can.
* Remove can from freezer and tape a design to the can with masking tape.
* Be sure to use a solid surface. Next lay the can on a folded towel and punch out the design by using a nail. Remove the paper and tape. Let the ice melt enough so that it can be removed from the tin can easily.
* Place the lantern upside down on a protected surface and spray with spray paint. Let dry. Make sure you are spraying the paint in a well-ventilated area. Place a small candle in the lantern.

On the FIFTH Day of

Christmas

We bring to you with love . . .

A Handkerchief Doll and a Sock Monkey! This is a doll just like your great-grandmother may have played with. They weren't able to go to the store and choose a doll off the shelf. These dolls were made from a man's white handkerchief, or sometimes they would use a woman's hanky. Today, these dolls are often made from hankies that have been handed down through the years and have become real treasures. In other words, they become keepsakes! I made dolls for you from hankies that once belonged to my mother, grandmother, and grandfather. Now they can be a keepsake for you. We made the sock monkeys for the boys in the family since they won't appreciate a "girlie" doll! We have included the book *Oscar: The Big Adventure of a Little Sock Monkey* by Leonard S. Marcus. It's such a great book and you will love having your own sock monkey after reading the story. Have fun with your new treasures. Each one of you is a treasure to us!

❄ ❄ ❄ ❄ ❄

I went through some boxes to find these special handkerchiefs I had been given when my grandmother and grandfather passed away and also ones that had belonged to my mother. I often wondered how I could display these hankies and not have them stuck away in a box. This was the perfect way to solve the problem. Again, this is an easy gift for mailing. The sock monkey dolls can be found in several discount stores in the toy department or, if you choose to make them, the pattern can be found on the Internet or in fabric stores.

Pattern for Making Hanky Dolls

* Use a standard man's white handkerchief, unfolded (a woman's hanky may be used).
* Fold in half and sew the two sides together, close to the hem, from the bottom edge about two-thirds of the way up the handkerchief.
* Turn right side out. Knot each of the two top corners close to the corner. This makes it look like a puffed sleeve with the corner sticking out for the arm.
* Place a wad of stuffing in the center between the two knots. Gather the material up around it and wind thread around it tightly several times and knot to form a head.
* Sew lace around the bottom of the "gown" and across the top of the head, making it look like a bonnet.
* Embroider a face on the doll, if you choose.

A similar doll can be made from a pillowcase. With a pillowcase, the sides are already sewn. Just knot the corners for arms, and follow instructions for handkerchief doll. If you have a pillowcase with lace or embroidery trim on the bottom, this will make a beautiful dress for your doll. Yarn can also be added for hair instead of lace for a bonnet.

On the SIXTH Day of

Christmas

We bring to you with love . . .

A Horse and Carriage Ride! Tonight is going to be a wonderful evening for our family! You are going on a horse and carriage ride just like children of the past would do. Bundle up so you will be toasty warm. We will bring blankets to cover your legs and feet. These December evenings can be very cold. We will sing some Christmas carols as we ride along and enjoy the spirit of this glorious holiday. We can hardly wait to spend time with you.

Our city has several horse-drawn carriages that take trips around town. The beautiful decorations can be seen and enjoyed, and it is a marvelous experience. We knew this was going to be an event the grandchildren would speak of for years to come. We hoped that they would think of their ancestors and how this was a common event for them during the holidays. They certainly couldn't jump in a car and drive around all cozy and warm while they looked at the holiday lights. If your town doesn't offer horse and carriage rides, perhaps you could locate a farm that has hayrides available. This could be lots of fun. Children love hayrides, and they could sing Christmas carols and make it a really fun evening. If you live away from your family, get on the Internet to see what their towns have to offer. It's so easy with modern technology today. If you find what you think would be fun for them, you could call ahead and get prices and availability. You may have to include one of the parents in your plan to make reservations so they won't be disappointed by not having time reserved. It will make a wonderful memory!

On the SEVENTH Day of

Christmas

We bring to you with love . . .

A New DVD! This DVD may be new to you, but it is a movie that has been around for many years. In fact, it is one of the most popular Christmas stories of all time. The movie is called *A Christmas Carol* and is a wonderful story written by Charles Dickens. We hope you will enjoy it together as a family. Maybe a batch of NeNa's fudge would be a perfect treat while you are enjoying your movie. Be listening for the doorbell. We love surprising you!

❄ ❄ ❄ ❄ ❄

Any Christmas DVD can be used, of course. We have always loved this one and felt it would work great for our family. There are lots of Christmas DVDs to choose from, so you're sure to find one that fits your family. This is a great gift for mailing—easy to wrap and light weight.

NeNa's Fudge

2 cups sugar

13 large marshmallows

2/3 cup evaporated milk

6 oz. chocolate chips

½ cup butter (not margarine)

1 tsp. pure vanilla

Nuts to taste

In a large skillet, mix together sugar, marshmallows, and evaporated milk. Dissolve and bring to a boil. While stirring constantly, time the mixture for *exactly 3 minutes* after boiling begins. Remove from heat and add the remainder of the ingredients. Stir until the butter and chocolate chips have melted well. Pour into a lightly buttered dish and refrigerate until cool.

On the EIGHTH Day of

Christmas

We bring to you with love . . .

A Christmas Tree for the Birds!! Have you ever thought about how the birds get their food during these cold winter days? Look outside your window and watch the birds flying among the bare branches of the trees, hoping that someone has thrown out a few crumbs or seeds for them. Today we are going to feed the birds! You all know how much PaPa loves the birds, and he makes sure he always has food out for them. Maybe he is Santa Claus to the birds! We have purchased a small fir tree and have placed it in a large pot in your yard. You are to place the bread, seeds, and nuts, which we have included, into the tiny baskets we purchased for you. Tie the baskets to the branches of the tree. Next, take some colorful ribbon and decorate the tree with bows. We have included some weatherproof ribbon in bright colors. At first the birds may not understand that this special tree is for them but soon some of the braver birds will venture to your tree. They will look around to make sure there is no danger. Other birds will come and they too will enjoy the food you have left for them. Be careful to not scare them away by moving too quickly around them or making noise. Also, make sure you keep the little baskets full of food for the birds. They will love you for being so good to them. This is definitely something our ancestors would do to make sure the little birds had food.

✳ ✳ ✳ ✳ ✳

If you are mailing your gifts, you'll need some help with this. I'm sure Mom or Dad would be happy to purchase the small tree for you and have it placed in a large pot. Have them understand that you want a small tree. You could send the seeds, nuts, colorful ribbon, or fabric strips along with very small baskets. Some families may already have a small tree in their yard that could be used. You might even include a book about birds so they can better recognize the birds in their area.

On the NINTH Day of
Christmas
We bring to you with love . . .

Stringing Popcorn and Cranberries! Another fun evening for you! Tonight we are coming to your house to string popcorn and cranberries just like the pioneers would do to make decorations for their trees. This will look great on the Christmas tree you use for hanging your memories. It's such fun knowing you have made the decorations yourself. Our ancestors couldn't shop in fancy stores and purchase beautiful ornaments and lights the way we can today. We hope you will think of our ancestors and remember the sacrifices they made for us. We remember them with love.

❋ ❋ ❋ ❋ ❋

This is truly a part of our past when we sit together and string popcorn and berries. We had lots of long needles and sturdy string for the family to use. They had a great time as we sat around their tree listening to Christmas music and making new decorations. We talked of our ancestors and how they paved the way for us, making our lives easier and richer. It's wonderful how there were records kept by the pioneers so we could know about their lives and how holidays were celebrated.

On the TENTH Day of
Christmas
We bring to you with love . . .

A Christmas Spider and Web! *Once upon a time, long ago, a gentle mother was busily cleaning the house for the most wonderful day of the year . . . the day on which the Christ Child came to bless the house. Not a speck of dust was left. Even the spiders had been banished from their cozy corner in the ceiling to avoid the housewife's busy leaning. They finally fled to the farthest corner of the attic.*

T'was Christmas Eve at last! The tree was decorated and waiting for the children to see it. But the poor spiders were frantic, for they could not see the tree nor be present for the Christ Child's visit. But the oldest and wisest spider suggested that perhaps they could peep through the crack in the door to see Him. Silently, they crept out of their attic, down the stairs, and across the floor to wait in the crack in the threshold. Suddenly, the door opened a bit and quickly the spiders scurried into the room. They must see the tree closely, since their eyes weren't accustomed to the brightness of the room . . . so they crept all over the tree, up and down, over every branch and twig, and saw every one of the pretty things. At last they satisfied themselves completely of the Christmas tree beauty.

But alas! Everywhere they went they had left their webs, and when the little Christ Child came to bless the house, He was dismayed. He loved the little spiders, for they were God's creatures too, but He knew the mother, who had trimmed the tree for the little children wouldn't feel the same, so He touched the webs and they all turned to sparkling, shimmering silver and gold! Ever since that time, we have hung tinsel on our Christmas trees, and according to the legend, it has been a custom to include a spider among the decorations on the tree.

Author Unknown

Isn't this a great story! We have a little toy spider, a decorative spider web, and some tinsel for you to place on your memory tree to remind you of the love of the Christ Child for all creatures. We have included some black paper, white yarn, and glue so that you can make some spider webs of your own. You might want to give one to a friend and include a copy of the story of the "Christmas Spider and Web." We have cut the black paper into squares so now you can use the glue to design a spider web and then carefully place the white yarn onto the glue. There are also some black plastic spiders and some tinsel for you to give away with the web. Have fun!

✳ ✳ ✳ ✳ ✳

This is a fun project for the children and one they can share with their friends for a special little Christmas gift. You can find the black spiders in just about any toy department of your local discount stores. The spider webs were found on an Internet site, but I think a craft store would carry something similar to the ones we found. If you are having trouble finding them, you might want to consider making your own. Be sure to add some glitter so your spider web will sparkle!

On the ELEVENTH Day of

Christmas

We bring to you with love . . .

A Christmas Maze! Years ago when our ancestors celebrated holidays, it was always with families getting together to share in the fun and excitement. Well, we are getting together again tonight to celebrate this glorious holiday with those we love so much. We are going to turn our family room into a game room for you to enjoy with all your cousins. We know this is one of your favorite things to do. There will be games that our ancestors would have played when they got together. One of the games we think you will enjoy most is called the Christmas Maze. Each one of you will be given a pencil with some yarn attached to it. You must follow the yarn until you reach the end and find the prize waiting for you. There will be lots of other games also. When NeNa and PaPa were young children, we played such games as "Tiddly Winks," "Jacks and Rocks," and "Pick-up Sticks." We'll have these games to play tonight, so be prepared for some stiff competition. We're pretty good! We can hardly wait until you arrive. Hurry!

❅ ❅ ❅ ❅ ❅

Give each player a pencil with a piece of yarn or string attached. Explain that each piece of yarn leads to a separate prize. Each player must wind the yarn on their pencil until they reach their prize. You will have previously hidden their prize somewhere in the room—under a chair or a cushion, in a drawer, a shoe or anywhere it can't be seen. Unwind the ball of yarn completely, passing it around table legs, under furniture and in and out of objects as you unwind. Don't worry about crisscrossing the yarn; that only makes the game more fun! Other fun games played by children of long ago are "Button, Button" and "Thimble, Thimble, Who's Got the Thimble." You'll think of others that will be lots of fun. I went on the Internet and got instructions for the maze game, and there were several others from which to choose.

On the TWELFTH Day of

Christmas

We bring to you with love . . .

A Wind–up Flashlight! What a fun way to pretend you are a pioneer! Go outside or turn the lights off in your house and pretend you don't have electricity and the only source of light is your flashlight. This can be a time when you will truly appreciate the luxuries you enjoy each day. You should keep your flashlight in a place where you can get to it quickly in case of an emergency. We all need to have a source of light readily available to us. Your wind-up flashlight doesn't need batteries, so it will always be ready when you need it. There is one for each member of your family.

❄ ❄ ❄ ❄ ❄

It's a good idea for every family to have a wind-up flashlight for each member of their family to use in times of emergency. Flashlights are a safe way of obtaining light. Batteries aren't always available or can go dead, so having at least one wind-up flashlight is a good idea. It gave us such a great feeling to know our families would have a source of light in case of a disaster. As I have said many times before, there is nothing quite as important to us as knowing our family is cared for and has what they might need.

Conclusion

Oh, how I have loved having you spend time with me in my Christmas room. It's very warm and cozy here and just the perfect place to share with friends like you. Memories fill my heart as I recall the past years of enriching the lives of our family with the 12 Days of Christmas. Every year brings more love and a stronger determination to provide a meaningful holiday season for those I love very much.

I often slip into my Christmas room and recall the faces of my precious grandchildren and their laughter as they hurried across the room to be the first one to complete the task and become the winner of the Amazing Race. I see those little Vaseline covered cheeks, noses, and eyebrows when they surfaced from a bucket filled with cotton balls, hoping to have collected more on their faces than any of their cousins. I remember the tenderness they expressed when they discussed a service project they had decided to do as a family and how excited they became as they talked of the children who had very little for Christmas who would now have some toys!

I recall the words of a dear lady who wrote to say she had found more happiness and joy through serving her family with the 12 Days of Christmas than she had ever known before. A picture fills my heart of Cameron and Beverly Hansen, a wonderful couple I met at the Conference Center, telling me how they made NeNa Butter together, the fun they had, and how delicious it was (the NeNa Butter recipe is on page 40 from my first book). A lady called to ask if the man in one of the stories in my book was from Wyoming? Could he be the same person she has been searching for these many years? Yes, it was indeed the same man and now the missing link in her genealogy was found. Where do you go to experience this kind of joy? I think of sweet Andrea Mylar from Aberdeen, Idaho, who prepared the 12 Days of Christmas not only for her children and grandchildren but also for her dear mother and father. They had such fun and felt such love. Andrea didn't know at the time that it would be her last Christmas spent with her father. Love was shown, lives were touched, and memories were embedded in their hearts forever. *We never know when final memories are being made.*

I learn of families who are now spending more time together during the holidays doing simple things that mean so much to their children. The smell of freshly baked cookies fills my mind, and I recall the stories of families who baked many hours to take these treats to people who perhaps weren't able to bake for themselves. These people knew someone cared for them. My heart is full of wonderful memories that I shall cherish forever. Isn't this exactly what Christmas is all about? It's the love we show for others in words and in deeds that reflect how we feel about our Savior. Can you imagine how Christ must feel when He sees us embracing the principles that He taught by the way He lived here on the earth? May we each strive to walk in His footsteps and prove worthy of His love.

I'll turn off the Christmas tree lights and the music and carefully place the Christmas books back in their stack. Then I'll take one last look at the pictures that will be embedded in my heart forever and say a silent prayer of thanksgiving for the memories that will carry me throughout the year. They will cause my heart to sing on many occasions. Never will there be a moment of regret for the time spent bringing more meaning to Christmas for my children and grandchildren. They truly are God's greatest gift. I look forward to spending time with my dear husband, who causes my heart to sing each day.

The door quietly closes on my Christmas room, but my heart will allow me to peek in every now and then, and each time I do, I'll smile. I'll be planning another fun year to present to our family with a meaningful theme chosen especially for them. My desire is that you too have chosen to make special memories with your children, grandchildren, parents, grandparents, relatives, and friends. Hopefully, there are ideas in this book that will get you started. If my ideas and suggestions aren't exactly what you want to do, then let them serve to get you thinking about what might suit your family best. I hope you are building your own Christmas room of beautiful memories. I'll be thinking of you.

> *And the Grinch, with his Grinch-feet ice cold in the snow, stood puzzling and puzzling, how could it be so? It came without ribbons. It came without tags. It came without packages, boxes, or bags. And he puzzled and puzzled till his puzzler was sore. Then the Grinch thought of something he hadn't before. What if Christmas, he thought, doesn't come from a store. What if Christmas, perhaps, means a little bit more.*

> Dr. Seuss

ACKNOWLEDGMENTS

A huge thank you to Cedar Fort Publishing, Inc., for once again allowing me to share my Christmas memories. You have made my dreams come true!

A special thank you to Joyce Kay Goodrich and Barbara Salsbury for listening with your hearts and being so willing to guide me through this. You are wonderful friends!

Gratitude fills my heart for my children, Kaye, Heather, Stephanie, Jason, Julie and Jon, and for my added blessings; Joe, Theron, Kelly, Justin, and Jill for continuing to believe in me and in the 12 Days of Christmas. You make each Christmas a priceless treasure and have given me more reasons for an "Encore." I love you more than ever!

To my beautiful grandchildren: Justin, Taylor, Cameron, Allison, Joseph, Nicholas, Vincent, Ethan, Jessica, Brianne, Rachel, Brooke, Nathan, Adam, Ashley, Andrew, Bowen, Austin, Olivia, Brynlee, Ellie, and Chloe—you truly light up my life! I thank God daily for you.

To the person who has believed in me completely—my wonderful husband, Sterling. I'll take over the household chores again, I promise! You are the answer to many prayers.

And to all who encouraged me to share the ideas from my Christmas room . . . thanks for believing in me. To Jackie Katuschenko, Harriett Sharpe, Lois Bady-Miller, and Carol Sue Kimble, never forget the depth of our friendship. You truly are angels in my life. And a very special thank you to a dear friend Mary Johnson, who had the courage to say to me, "Betty, you need to write a book!"

About the Author

Betty LaFon Van Orden was born in Cambria, Virginia. She attended school in Fairlawn and Dublin, Virginia; New Martinsville, West Virginia; and Brigham Young University in Provo, Utah.

Betty is a member of The Church of Jesus Christ of Latter-Day Saints and has served in many auxiliaries. Betty has also served on various committees in her community, helping to improve the guidelines and standards that govern the activities of high school students.

Betty and her husband, Sterling, are presently living in Syracuse, Utah. They are serving a three-year mission as supervisors of the Conference Center in Salt Lake City. They have six children and twenty-two grandchildren. Betty is the author of *The Twelve Days of Christmas—Ideas for a More Meaningful Holiday Season.*